GOLDEN HORIZON

"DELIGHT YOURSELF IN THE LORD AND HE WILL GIVE YOU THE DESIRES OF YOUR HEART."
PSALM 37:4

Danniel Campbell

Golden Horizon
Copyright © 2016 by **Danniel Campbell**.
All rights reserved.

No part of this publication may be reproduced, stored in a retrieval system or transmitted in any way by any means, electronic, mechanical, photocopy, recording or otherwise, without the prior permission of the author except as provided by USA copyright law.

All characters appearing in this work are fictitious. Any resemblance to real persons, living or dead, is purely coincidental.

The opinions expressed by the author are not necessarily those of Revival Waves of Glory Books & Publishing.

Published by Revival Waves of Glory Books & Publishing
PO Box 596| Litchfield, Illinois 62056 USA
www.revivalwavesofgloryministries.com

Revival Waves of Glory Books & Publishing is committed to excellence in the publishing industry.

Book design copyright © 2016 by Revival Waves of Glory Books & Publishing. All rights reserved.

Paperback: 978-0692736531

Hardcover: 978-1-68411-161-9

Published in the United States of America

Table of Contents

Chapter ONE 4
Chapter TWO 8
Chapter THREE 20
Chapter FOUR 26
Chapter FIVE 34
Chapter SIX 41
Chapter SEVEN 46
Chapter EIGHT 54
Chapter NINE 60
Chapter TEN 70
Chapter ELEVEN 75
Chapter TWELVE 81
Chapter THIRTEEN 89
Chapter FOURTEEN 96
Chapter FIFTEEN 101
Chapter SIXTEEN 108
Chapter SEVENTEEN 115
Chapter EIGHTEEN 122
Chapter NINETEEN 126
Chapter TWENTY 130
Chapter TWENTY ONE 132
Chapter TWENTY TWO 139
Chapter TWENTY THREE 147
Chapter TWENTY FOUR 152
Chapter TWENTY FIVE 156
Chapter TWENTY SIX 165
Chapter TWENTY SEVEN 167

CHAPTER ONE

It was 2:00 p.m. that late Spring Saturday afternoon at the renown Circuit de la Sarthe, on the country side of Le Mans, France. Spectators awaiting the race to come were swarming about the track buying all sorts of souvenirs and getting autographs from their favorite racers, while most of the competing teams were trying to squeeze out as much last minute tweaks and strategy they could muster. A few of the competitors, however gathered and huddled in prayer in a particular garage. After everyone in the group had requested everything they needed and wanted from the Lord, a tall slender older man closed out the time of prayer saying, "Again we ask You, Jesus to empower us to represent You well on the track this weekend. May Your favor be on us for victory and that You give us the perseverance we need to finish this very grueling competition. Your will be done." With that he said amen and everyone broke away to their respected garages.

In the midst of the dispersing competitors stood a very tall dark man in a white, gold and blue striped fire suit. He was also a very big man, in fact with muscles as sound as oak wood, and skin as black as the night's cloak. After the Dark Giant shook one of the leaving racers' hands he looked around at the conversations of the other teams' garages. He was just starting to grow in spirit gazing at the thousands upon thousands of spectators in the stands blowing their kazoos, honking their horns, and waving almost every nations' banner. *I can't believe I've been gone from this for so long.* Though this question was not posed on purpose, he unintentionally answered it by traveling back to what he considered the darkest hour of his life. As his mind lingered there for a moment he only felt a little guilt, but it was when he returned his eyes to the crowds that he formed the memory into a dagger. His once proud broad face took a mud slide. *I don't deserve this* said he to the Lord with his heart, "Why did you even give this back to me?" All the real sounds around him were drowned out with the mental stabs of condemnation, *That's right; You don't deserve to be here. You almost cursed God. You're selfish. You made racing an idol.*

He then heard a voice cut through the mental smog. He knew it came from outside of his head, but he couldn't make out what was said.

"What was that?" asked the Dark Giant.

"I said you're not getting the pre-race jitters now are you, Cody?" asked the voice from behind. "Especially since we just prayed."

Cody's head was lowered to the floor with his hands resting on his hips. "No, Chief." He answered with a wag of his head. "No, I just got a feeling of guilt that hit me all of a sudden, that's all."

"What do you mean, guilt?" Hearing a tone of alarm in his voice Cody looked over to the man. His friend's bushy gray brows lowered almost to the silver rims of his glasses, staring him with small blue eyes of unease. He was a dear old friend to Cody. Rick Gora was his real name, but he preferred calling him Chief, since he was the last crew chief of his late father. "You told me Jesus was fine with you racing again. Was that true?"

"Yeah. I mean, I didn't get any push back from Him when I figured He was telling me I could return. I didn't feel any resistance from Him at any point from the time we built the car till now."

"So what's making you feel it now?"

Cody shrugged his shoulders. "I just got to looking around seeing the people cheering, the engines starting, the engineers gabbing, the must of diesel and gasoline. Just hit me all of a sudden." Cody lowered his head again. "After how I treated Him for all those years… I'm just starting to realize now that I'm not worthy of any of this."

"That's the point, Kodiak," said Rick, "you're not worthy of this and it's not about you. That's what you realized five years ago before we got here, today, right?" His friend then firmly grasped his shoulders as he came around and stood before him staring him eye to eye. Rick was only a couple of inches shorter than him with a build far inferior, but his spirit within, though calm, was sincere, and Cody knew he sought the truth. "So is coming back to this sport about Him, or you?"

Cody searched his heart to see if it was, and when he believed it was pure he did not feel the Lord's scorn. "Yeah, it's about Him."

"Did you come back for Him?"

"Yeah."

Cody felt his engineer's grip tighten on his shoulders with a flint-like stare. "Then enjoy the grace that He's given you."

Cody nodded his head. He then shook Rick's hand and hugged him. "Thanks, Chief."

After Cody had been buckled into his seat in his car Rick knelt down leaning his head into the cockpit, "Now remember, your first stint here is all about aggression. Gas, gas all the way. You know because of fuel, distance and velocity's our edge. We need at least a near lap lead on the competition before you come in for fuel."

"Right, Chief."

They both then prayed again to the Lord for theirs, as well as their competitors' protection. With that Rick gently tapped him on the head while stepping away from the car.

"Let's go get 'em." said Rick as he shut the door. Cody then pulled down his gold chrome visor, and after the last car left from its garage and went past him, he followed it down pit lane.

CHAPTER TWO

In most European and American endurance racing series, such as the Rolex Sports Car Series, there are different tiers, or classes competing simultaneously on the track. The International Nurburgring/I.N. Series had three tiers; Tiers 2 and 3 were reserved for race ready sports cars such as a Corvette or a Porsche 911, but Tier 1 was reserved for cars that you would only find on a race track, like a Formula One car. And why would a Tier One belong only on a track, you might ask? Well, again let's say you happen to see a modern generation Porsche or Corvette. You'll notice that they are far wider and lower to the ground than say a Ford Taurus, or a Mercedes C Class sedan. Well, imagine a car even wider and so low to the ground that you'd swear it would crush pebbles. Then take away what would normally be a front bumper and a grill, and replace it with a beak and wing underneath. Also the bodies of these cars are framed around the driver like a cockpit with all sorts of winglets, wings, and ducts to keep the car stuck to the ground at high speeds, as well as suck and channel the surrounding air to disclosed instruments like engines, radiators, and brake discs to keep them cool.

Now most of these Tier One machines had relatively disappointing sounds that were contrary to their daunting presences, for they were all mostly powered by small displaced hybrid engines fueled with diesel and electricity.

Even the larger hybrid diesel engines, such as the V8s or V12s would lose to the acoustics of a vacuum cleaner.

But the Judgment, Cody's carbon-fibered chariot of choice, was completely alien to such frills. Its full name, the Judgment AWD R 10V20 stood for all-wheel-drive-steering race spec., with a ten liter V-shaped 20 valve engine. It was not a few inches wider and longer than any in its tier, for Cody was pretty much bigger and taller than any driver in the league, or any other racing league for that matter, and the engine was fairly larger than any of the others. From an above view, its body curved around the cockpit until both sides joined at the front making a large very-pointed nose. That nose then had a large wing underneath, called a splitter, and there were two enormous ducts behind both sides of the nose. On both edges of each splitter where very large ominous circled headlights that were molded into the fenders. The cockpit was a near flat bubble with a double humped surface, and flanking the sides of the cockpit were two huge scope-like ducts that sucked air into the engine at high speeds. The car's beak and cockpit surfaces had little winglets that extended out, and on its side panels were all sorts of ducts and gills in means to avail itself of the wrath of lifting gales. Also, unlike its competitors, its rear wing was disclosed allowing for far higher speeds than theirs. However, whenever the car had to stop from speeds 210 miles per hour/mph or higher its enormous black wing would swiftly extend from the rear giving the car enough down force to be stable through the turns.

Most race cars are usually painted in one color or multi-toned with a lot of their sponsors' decals hand sketched over them. But the Judgment was very unique in this area, too. The front half of the car had a pearl-scent flare of white and orange fire painted over it with bolts of blue and white lightening streaking behind fading into streams of white lines, stars, and many colored novas speckled over space on the back half.

And the menacing sound it made. It's only disadvantage to its other Tier One combatants was that its engine was petroleum fueled instead of diesel. Since petrol burns quicker than diesel it had more pit stops giving the competition some hope against the beast, but with that deficit came a deep visceral roar that would make even a volcano chirp.

Once all the competing cars arrived at their respected positions behind the starting line, the pace car emerged before the leading car having all the vehicles trail it around the circuit. Cody's bowls now were like confetti being whisked in a crucible, and as each passing turn and straight away brought him closer and closer to the starting line it only deepened. The Dark Giant loved to chase rather than being chased, but since he had pole all the pressure was on him to maintain the lead. Hunting down the leader always gave him the adrenaline he needed to go faster than he would usually deem possible, but since his 1450 horse power Judgment obliterated every tiers' time, he wondered just what his push would be. As he looked to and fro at all the cheering spectators and canopies strewn along behind the cement barriers of the straight leading to the Ford Chicanes, he knew the race start was just seconds away. As the pace car in front left into pit lane, Cody recalled what his high school weightlifting coach told him, "Beat you Cody. You're the opponent, not the other lifter."

That's what I'll do he thought. *Since I'm in front I'll just race against myself.* After he cleared the chicanes he could see all the white position brackets leading up to the starting line.

"French flag," heard Cody through his ear piece. "French flag." He then mashed down on the accelerator, and in a bolt of terrifying thunder flew past the Michillen stand to the Dunlap chicane darting under the famous giant tire overpass. He snaked up and down through the elbow shaped Esses until he tapped on the brakes coming into the Tetre Rouge hair pin turn.

Once he finally emerged on the Mulsanne Straight the Judgment, as it had done during his practice and qualifying laps stole the Dark Giant's heart. In a cacophony of earthquakes it shot down the two mile plus straight away. Now Cody had always preferred ANSCA (Acronym for American National Sports Car Association) powerful front-engine sport cars over the mid-engine ones in endurance races. He loved taming the boisterous and twitchy V8 up front, rather than forgoing the propelling of a V8 or V12 from behind, but for Cody taming the Judgment was more satisfying. So frightening was the sound behind him, as well as the near warp-speed acceleration, that he thought his 6'8 and 290 lbs. physique was more like a moth being flung by the hand of God. He felt almost completely helpless as he held on to his little steering wheel that flashed green, yellow, and red with each clip of the shifting paddles behind it. But all he could do was smile. He would have screamed in ecstasy of the immense sum of asphalt, trees, and houses his car passed if it were not for him having to keep the radio chatter clear for his engineer.

In a back fire Cody was coming into the hairpin Mulsanne Turn. He took his foot off the accelerator, and with just a tap on the brake pedal dropped the Judgment's enormous chrome gold, ceramic brake calipers on the wheels lowering its speed from 330 mph to 100 in seconds. The car's rear wing then parachuted up, and it's combined down force with the front splitter made it suck down to the road tighter than an octopus' grip. The winglets, fins, and ducts too worked in helping disperse and channel the immense air it generated, as well as the rear wheels steering opposite the front. All this gave Cody enough g-force to scalpel through the apex and out of the turn in a breath.

By the end of the second lap, Cody was coming out of the Arnage turn when he heard Rick over his helmet's ear piece say, "Traffic ahead." He then noticed several red break lights of some Tier Three and Two cars ahead of him coming into the Porsche Curves. It was then that Cody was reminded that there were actually 54 other cars on the track. Due to the Judgment's dominance on the straights and turns, it had been several minutes since he had seen any other evidence that there were others, besides him, competing in the race. In fact, the last he saw any car behind or in front was when he pulled up to his position on the grid and during his first trip down the Mulsanne.

"How much traffic I got coming my way, Chief?" asked Cody through his helmet's speaker.

There came a silence, which the Dark Giant had already anticipated. He knew that his engineer would have to pause to look at the location of the cars' blips on the digital track map in the garage monitor. After blowing past several cars down the Dunlop Curve, his engineer answered, "The congestion's mostly on the Tetre Rouge and the beginning of the Mulsanne, and the 2nd place Raffinatos are just entering the Mulsane turn. Give it four minutes or so, and if the Tier Ones ahead don't give you any trouble you should be nipping on their red heels."

As Cody returned unto the Mulsanne Straight for the third time he flashed his bright lights for the sea of much slower cars blocking his way. As the automotive waters parted, the Dark Giant galloped his cosmic-skinned beast right on through. Within several minutes, just as Rick predicted, Cody met the rears of the three wine-red Raffinatos coming into the Indianapolis turn. Believing the straggler of the pack was there to ward him off, Cody knew he had to be cunning to finagle himself beside him. He then poked his car to the left hoping the opponent in front would go the same direction thinking to block him. He did. As soon as the straggling Raffinato veered to the left, Cody switched to the right, and since they both were coming into the Porsche Turns, Cody knew his opponent wouldn't have enough grip to rebound. He then slipped in and flanked him through the long chicanes. Cody followed the Raffinato in front of him line for line and turn for turn. He did not have the space to overtake him due to the other two cars that were beside and in front of him, but he allowed no gap between him and his competitor hoping the pressure would convince the driver to make way.

The four of them finally arrived on the Mulsanne.

"Cody," said Rick, "someone busted a tire and they're snailing a hundred yards ahead. Ease up. That'll give the guy up front the margin of era."

Cody did as ordered, letting his foot up off the gas allowing about a four foot gap between him and the one upfront. A few seconds later, he saw between the Raffinatos the wounded car up ahead crawling with its near bald wheel sparking against the asphalt. Suddenly, the flailing strip of rubber from the car's wheel whipped at its rear bumper knocking it off its hinge. As soon as it scraped the asphalt it popped off, and since all this happened so quickly, the Raffinato directly in front of Cody overcorrected swerving completely off the track into the well paved red dirt. Steering free from the limping car, the Dark Giant pulled up ahead. When he glanced over to the opponent beside him he saw him banging his steering wheel with his fist.

"Ha." Cody understood his contender's frustration. No one wants to be a lap down. No one. But his excitement from the chance God provided him to get ahead outweighed his empathy. "Thank you, Jesus," he said while pumping a fist to Him in the air.

"That ah a boy, Johnson," said Rick. "Good driving."

CHAPTER THREE

Within five laps after his first fuel stop Cody had lapped the Raffinatos again, putting Team Judgment two laps ahead of every Tier One competitor. He then stuck to his initial strategy for the remainder of his first two hour stint; defeating himself. After his thirteenth lap he would ask Rick what his time was.

"Rick." Cody would ask.

"Yeah?" Rick would answer.

"What's my time?"

"2:57."

"Rick?"

"Yeah?"

"Time?"

"2:56."

"Chief?"

"2:55."

"Time?"

"2:53."

He grinned with every second gained, but with each second lost he made it his motivation to go even harder. He attacked every turn with a vengeance, and chased every straight as if trying to catch himself. By the end of his first stint, Cody had absolutely dominated the competition. He was five laps ahead of the Raffinatos, and had nearly eight on the slower Tier Threes and Twos.

"Alright, Johnson," said his engineer. "Time to pass the baton."

A few seconds later the Dark Giant pulled into pit lane. As he rolled by all the cars and the flocks of men in fire suits attending them, Cody noticed his post man just several feet ahead. On a dime's envy he stopped before the white plastic post with the car's name written in silver, and was immediately swarmed by his own men. He then hauled himself out of the Judgment while his pit team air jacked the car for refueling and tire changes.

As soon as he stepped back and took off his glossed white and platinum striped helmet, his ears were flooded by the full volume of the commotion around him. Excitement's lava was swirling within, and seeing Eloi Amedee, one of his two co-drivers, slip into the cockpit after him almost turned it into loathing. If it wasn't for the regulations, and shear common sense, he would have stretched his first two hours to maybe four or five. He then leaned in buckling his teammate in his seat.

"Make 'em burn, baby!" shouted the Dark Giant to Eloi with a slap on his helmet.

As the crew men released the air jack, he saw Eloi nod his head while reaching up to close the hatch. The post man then jumped out of the way leaving the Judgment to head down pit road.

"You sure did give us a hard act to follow, big man!" Cody heard Iarlaith Dennison, his other co-driver yell as he approached him.

"Just following the One who gave me the ability to put it on!" answered Cody through his ski mask.

"Don't you take credit for anything?!"

"Only for the bad stuff!" Cody gave him a soft buck on the head with his and high-fived him. "Woo!!" he shouted swinging his right fist in enthusiasm. He then gazed at the whole pit crew while approaching them. "You guys put the Q in quick out there!" He gave them all high-fives and hugs, but he noticed he had made many of them anxious.

"Butterbomb." He felt someone's hand pat him on the back. "This ain't American football. These European types are a little stoic when it comes to encouragement. They're not used to big, emotional, black men shouting and dapping 'em up."

"Oh yeah?" said Cody as he turned around. He then looked down at his younger sister, who was only a few inches shorter than him yet with skin nearly as tanned as his. Algoma was her name, a very comely young woman with large violet eyes and shiny, thick, long black hair.

Cody then bobbled his head in mock anger. "Well it's about time they start getting used to it, Possum.

"Ain't no stoic behavior tolerated in my garage," he immediately looked away to one of his pit crew members, "right, Pablo!" The much smaller man nodded in agreement. Cody then gave a playful laugh, while giving him a soft pound on his shoulder with his fist. He turned to his sister and gave her a peck on her forehead.

"Good job, Kodiak," she said as he walked away.

As Cody headed over to Rick, he overheard him say to Eloi through his mouth piece, "It's all about maintaining the lead right now for you, Amedee. Just keep it smooth and tight."

He grasped the back of his old friend's shoulders while looking up at the race footage on one of the monitors above.

"Good run, Cody," said his engineer. "You've given us a lot of cushion."

"Two hours down," said Cody, "Twenty-two more to go."

Through the lucid night till the down pouring dawn, Team Judgment kept their lead all throughout. God allowed no accidents, nor the weather to hinder them. As the clock finally struck zero, and with still 20 laps ahead on the second place Raffinato, Iarlaith had just the Ford chicanes to cross before coming to the crown. As he watched the Judgment cross the finish line, Cody grinned while holding out his hand to Rick. Rick took hold, and Cody hugged him to his side.

"I'd say this is God's absolute confirmation for phase one of the ministry, eh Chief!" said Cody grasping his engineer's shoulders.

"Amen to that!" said Rick with a smile. "He couldn't have made it any clearer!"

CHAPTER THREE

Team Judgment won much with their victory at the 24 hours of La Sarthe. However, above the all the money and acclaim acquired from the win the most valuable prize attained was a partnership with Usangi-Kon, Japan's most distinguished privately owned racing manufacturer. Known for their string of victories in Veloce Formula and Moto GT, they were looking to join forces in next year's International Nurburgring season with the best performing independent manufacturer for the whole 24 hours of La Sarthe. And being the victor of the International Nurburgring's most prominent event Team Judgment had absolutely earned their hand in comradery.

On the windy and cloudy Monday afternoon following their win, Cody and some of the members of his team were discussing the details of their partnership with Usangi-Kon Racing's executive staff at a restaurant in downtown Le Mans. After the team owners all signed the contract they shook each other's hands and bowed in respect. However, as Cody held out his hand to one of the other team members he just walked off and left with the others out of the door. The Dark Giant raised his eyebrow.

"What's his deal?" said Rick who was standing behind Cody.

"Don't know," answered Cody. "He was sour the whole time, though."

"Yeah," said Algoma with a tap on her brother's arm, "sour from the taste of *black lemons*."

"You gotta point there, Goma." chimed Lope Celso, team Judgment's chief of aero-dynamics.

Cody went through the door and held it for everyone to go through. As he was heading back down the alley to their rented white Mercedes, he heard a woman's voice calling from behind.

"Cody!"

"Hm." The Dark Giant stopped and turned as the others continued on.

"Cody, I'd like a word with you!"

When he saw who the voice belonged to, his broad flat face glowed. "What's up Ms. Diego?"

"Oh, don't call me that," she said as she stopped before him gently tapping his arm. "Just call me by my first name."

"Okay, Catherina. What's up?"

"I never got the chance to tell you how moved I was by the reasons you gave at the pre-race interviews for why you race, being a child of Christ myself…"

A Christian thought Cody as his eyebrows rose. He wanted to make a response to this charming reality, being that he now knew they were both of the same faith, but believing it would be too awkward to state his interest now, he instead interjected, "You were there at the press conference?"

"All of us were. You didn't have a huge impact on Michi, though."

"Oh," he gave a look of facetious surprise. "Why's that?"

Catherina beamed him a warm smile as the wind filmed her raven black hair over her long oval face. "Oh, he's just your typical racist."

"Ah, ha." Cody nodded his head. "That would definitely explain why he didn't shake my hand like the rest of your crew."

"Yeah. Anyway, as I was trying to say before, after the V. F. season is finished in November my family and I are going down to Central America to do some evangelism. We could use someone of your zeal to accompany us, unless you have other plans during that time."

Cody grasped his chin in thought.

"Oh, tonto de mí." She raised her sun glasses unto her forehead. Her now exposed thin brown eyes rolled in annoyance.

"What's wrong?" asked Cody.

Catherina held the back of her scalp in concern. "That'll probably be a problem for you, huh papi?"

"What would?"

"Being surrounded by all those non-English speaking people?"

"I can speak Spanish, if that's what you mean."

She raised one of her thick eyebrows. "Really?"

"Yeah. I speak it fluently."

Catherina smirked with guile as she folded her arms. "Fluently?"

"Like water," said Cody with his right arm held high.

He could see she still doubted him as she chuckled. She stroked her hair behind her shoulder and asked in Spanish, "So when did you start learning to speak it?"

"Since seventh grade," returned Cody, with a smile in her tongue,

Catherina flashed a toothy grin as her once fair face was blotted scarlet. She continued in Spanish, "You can't be serious."

"Like a hernia," quipped Cody in her tongue, "but if you want to run more tests like this I'd be eager to oblige."

"Okay, okay." She returned her tongue to English while waving her hand in surrender. She again put her flapping hair in back of her shoulder. "You Dominican?"

"Nope. African American and half Native American Indian, to be exact."

For a moment the two of them just stared at each other. They felt the warmth of something like a small sun grow between them. The fact that Cody was so attracted to her perplexed him. He naturally preferred women of tall and wide stature, but Catherina was more than a foot shorter than him and had a slender physique. However, a sweet face and lovely hair always hooked him more, and what rested above his host's stature was clear enough for the blind to see.

"We can't wait forever, flirt!" yelled a voice from behind Catherina.

As Cody looked up to see who the rude speaker was, Catherina sighed. When he returned his eyes to hers her face became cold as she took her little leather tangerine purse from her shoulder.

"It's a ten minute ride back to the hotel, Squid." said Catherina. "If you want it to be a pleasant one then zip it!" She looked back up at Cody while groping through her purse. "Apparently my engineer thinks he can manage my conversations too. I've held them up long enough, though." She then took out her large flat phone and pen. "Why don't we exchange email addresses if you're interested."

"Sure." Cody pulled his phone out of his pocket, flipping it open. "I don't think I've got anything planned for September, or October." They both inputted each other's contacts in their devices.

"I'll shoot you an email when I get to the hotel." She then held out her hand and Cody shook it. "God bless."

"God bless you too," said Cody with a nod as he watched her wave with a huge smile. "Safe travels."

She turned around and hurriedly walked towards her employer's car as her very long black hair flailed free like a cape. Cody's eyes glittered in delight of her, and to keep his thoughts shepherded within the realm of innocence he immediately turned away. As he headed for the car he saw both his friends and his sister standing by the Mercedes grinning with what looked like suspicion.

Great. He wagged his head while digging his hand in his pocket. *Here we go.* "What?" he asked while pulling out his keys. The smiles were still smeared on their faces as he clicked open their doors. "What?"

"Getting a little *amiable* with your partner, eh Kodiak?" said his sister in a dainty pose. "Probably why you let us all stand out here being as you were too *occupied* to open the door for us?"

"Come on, Possum," said Cody while plopping in the driver's seat. Rick and Lope snickered while bowing into the car. "We were only talking about future ministry opportunities. We weren't checking our calendars for a date. Can't a cat just be a cat?"

"Yeah," his sister answered while sitting in the passenger seat, "if the cat's actually a cat."

"Whatever." Cody smirked while shaking his head, as he turned over the ignition.

CHAPTER FOUR

During the week of Thanksgiving, Cody's mother, Nadie had come up from her missionary work on an Arapaho Reserve in Wyoming to visit him and Algoma for the holiday at their family home in Cotulla, Texas. That Thursday afternoon, they all cooked a huge feast and gathered at the kitchen table to eat. As soon as they had finishing saying grace his mother immediately asked him and his sister, "So are you two seeing anyone right now?"

The Dark Giant shook his head in annoyance.

"Not me," his sister answered.

"How come?"

"I'm just not interested in having anyone right now."

"There aren't any impressionable bachelors in the church or around Lerado for you?"

"Nah. Have you taken a liking to anyone at the rez, yet?"

"Ho, ho okay." Cody took a fork full of turkey while glancing up, and saw the devious grin on Algoma's face.

"So you flipped it on me now, eh," his mother continued. "Well, I'd say the answer for me is the same as yours." Nadie looked up while tapping the air with her empty fork. "Quite frankly, I don't ever plan on looking for another."

"I hope it's not age that's holding you back," said Algoma.

"No, no. It's nothing to do with that." Nadie took a sip of wine while still holding her eyes to the ceiling. "I'm just content with not being in that kind of relationship again, that's all. It requires a huge investment into a person, you know. When your father died, it was like a huge spiritual stock crash for me, and it took the Lord a long moon to fill the deficit." She returned her eyes to his sister with a sincere stare, shaking her head softly. "I don't think I could weather that again. I'm just not willing to take the risk."

"Hey mom, I didn't mean to upset..."

"What're you talking about, Goma?" She then tapped his sister softly on her arm with a strong *never mind* expression. "Smokey's been gone for years, honey. God's healed that wound in time." After a couple seconds of silence his mother's high cheeks dimpled again while digging her fork into some collard greens. "How 'bout you, Kodiak?"

"Oh, you ain't pulling me into this," said Cody while wiping his face with his napkin.

"You didn't think you'd evade the relationship grill, too did you, bro?" said his sister with that same mischievous sneer.

"Yeah I can." He nodded in certainty while taking a fork full of mash potatoes.

She then whispered to their mother, "He's been digitally courting this little Hispanic race car driver. Catherina, I think her name is."

Cody shook his head in denial, straining hard to mask the grin emerging.

"You mean my Kodiak's finally getting the Latina girl he's always wanted?"

"You better take your daughter with you when you go back to Wyoming," said Cody. "She might not live long enough till your next visit."

"You were going to keep all this from me, weren't you?" asked Nadie.

"First of all," he playfully pointed his fork full of turkey at his sister, "She's not some racer. She's the lead driver of the team we've partnered with."

"Don't worry." His sister nipped from her fork. "I understand you two have to keep things *professional*."

Wagging his head, he turned to his mother. "She's our new main ally on the track for the next season in the International Nurburgring series."

"And that's as far as your relationship goes with her?" asked his mother in great eagerness.

His sister then leaned forward with both elbows on the table cuffing her chin in her hands, while staring him in humorous anticipation.

Cody glanced down to fork up another mouth full of greens. As he chewed he glanced back up at his family and was surprised that they had actually stopped eating in expectation. "Should have gone to Poland with Rick for Thanksgiving and Christmas. Could have avoided this prying altogether." He tried to maintain his glee while returning his eyes to the plate.

"Oooh, are those dimples I see forming," said his sister.

"Is she a Christian?" asked his mother.

"Yeah," answered Cody with a nod.

"Do you have a picture of her?"

"Yeah." Cody didn't say anything further hoping his mother wouldn't pry anymore and continued eating, but he could still feel the subtle energy of her staring him for more information.

"Well, where is it?" his mother asked.

"Where's what?"

"The picture?"

Cody shook his head in defeat while rising up from the table. He then waved his hand for her to follow him, and both Nadie and Algoma got up walking behind him. The three of them stopped before the computer at the snug gray cubicle in the middle of the hallway, and Cody leaned down pressing the sleep button to bring it on. He then went in his email and showed them a photo Catherina had sent him of her cheering with her first place trophy on the podium at the Grando Primio Do Brazil race.

"She's so pretty, Cody," said his mother with a great smile.

"Wait till you see this," said Algoma as she typed up YOUTUBE in the web browser.

Cody stood confused wondering what she was up to until she pulled up Catherina's Pantene-Pro V commercial.

"Wow, Kodiak," said Nadie. "You've got a real hawk's eye for splendor. If she was a foot taller she'd be a perfect fit for Pocahontas."

"We're only trying to get to know each other right now, mom."

"She's stopping by here this Monday to pick him up," said his sister, while clasping her hands behind their mother's shoulders. "They're going to fly to Central America for a mission's trip."

"You've always been the mouth for my mind," said Cody facetiously while looking away.

"Someone's gotta be its voice," said his sister giving him a light tap on the forehead.

"Well, praise the Lord, Cody," said his mother with a pat on the chest. "That's just wonderful. Now why is she coming here to pick you up? You can't just fly there on your own?"

"Well, she always comes to Dallas around this time of year to see her sister Ercilia's car in an auto show outreach. They call it Tuner Tabernacle, I believe."

"Tuner Tabernacle," his mother interjected. "I like that."

"Yeah, well she figured it would be better for her and her sister to swing down here to get me and have all of us head up together to the airport in Laredo. We'll fly out for Honduras from there."

"This'll be a great time for you to meet her, momma," said his sister.

"Possum," said Cody holding out his hands in annoyance.

"That sounds great, Goma," said their mother. "I can't wait to see her."

That coming Monday, Catherina and her sister, Ercilia, arrived at the Johnsons' home and spent a few hours eating and talking with the family before they left for the airport. As Cody finished putting the last of his luggage in Ercilia's S.U.V., the women were still busy chatting away amongst each other. Cody, however, just folded his arms and rested his back on the passenger's side door waiting for them to finish. Ercilia then finally glanced back and noticed him waiting. She then softly elbowed her older sister in the rib, and when Catherina turned her head to her to see what she wanted; she pointed her thumb back towards him.

"Oh, I'm sorry Cody," said Catherina when she turned around. "You've been ready all this time?"

"Oh, about fifteen minutes," he answered with a smirk, "give or take."

"Well, why didn't you say something?" asked Ercilia.

"Well momma always taught me that it was criminal for men to interrupt women during their bantering."

"Whatever," said Catherina shooing him with her hand while the other women rolled their eyes sighing.

As Cody came up he watched the four women hug and kiss each other goodbye.

He then stepped forward and hugged his sister. "Bye Possum."

"Bye Butterbomb," she quipped with her mischievous grin.

"Don't call me that in front them," whispered an embarrassed Cody to his sister as he gave her a soft elbow on the shoulder.

He then leaned down and hugged his mom. "You take care, Kodiak," said his mom while kissing him on the cheek. She then held on to his jaw whispering, "I think that Catherina's a ripe pick for you. You hold on to her, now, you hear."

Cody paused relishing the joy in his mother's eyes.

"What's wrong, dear?"

"Nothing." He smiled. "I'm just enjoying you finally being happy for where I'm going this time." He then pecked her on her forehead with his lips, and walked off to the S.U.V. As he hopped into the backseat Catherina beeped and waved goodbye to his family, and with that the three of them drove off down the long dirt road.

CHAPTER FIVE

A week after he arrived in Central America, Cody, the Diegos, along with some of their friends and family were all traveling the forest roads of Nicaragua in their Range Rover behind another ministry van. Cody sat in much enjoyment of the ride as he gazed out the window at the pale turquoise sea sparkling through the trees. He didn't even mind the frequent bumps jolting him in the behind from the muddy road they traversed.

"So far today's been much smoother than the last two," said Cody to Catherina, who was at the wheel.

"Yeah," added a small middle aged man in the passenger seat, "a little too smooth for me."

"What do you mean by that, Papa?" asked Catherina.

"I can't help but feel that violence is inevitable here."

"I thought the gangs didn't hang around this spot often?" said one of Catherina's cousins.

"Never and often are two drastically different things, Gasper," answered Catherina's father.

"We all knew the risks of coming here, Fermi," said an older woman sitting directly in front of Cody. "These peoples' need for the Word outweighs our safety. Satan's demonic stronghold through violence in this region is what he hopes will prevent us from bringing the Word to them, but to live is Christ and to die is gain."

"I know, I know my dear," said Fermi to his wife while looking out the window. "I've just had my fair share of murder and bloodshed from growing up here, that's all. I would regret if anything happened to you all, the other missionaries, or the very people we're trying to minister to."

The party in the van softly bumped about in their seats in silence as the vehicle continued down the road. After the quiet had continued, Cody glanced up and saw Catherina's reflection as she was looking up at the rear view mirror.

"Why don't we pray to the Lord for His protection, and that His Word be preached with boldness?" Everyone in the van agreed to do so, and they all started praying.

When they finally arrived at the beach, many of the staff went out two by two around the villages in the forest to gather adults and their children to come to their location, while a few of them remained behind on the beach to prepare the equipment for the object lesson and activities. After the mission teams had assembled all the villagers who wanted to come they began to entertain the children with illusion tricks and games themed around the Gospel.

At some point during the festivities Cody, who was sitting amongst the crowd of children on the blue tarp, heard some commotion from behind. When he turned his head to the noise, he saw a rambunctious group of youths and young men emerge from the trees afar on the other side of the beach. As the other group sat in the sand, Cody asked the other ministry leader sitting beside him, "Are those the gangs we were informed of?"

The missionary scooted around to look at those Cody was referring to. "Yep." He nodded in agreement. "That's them."

While a few of the male gang members where horsing around, one of them, who was standing quietly by himself, turned and stared in what seemed like great interest towards Cody's direction. The gangster, with hesitant steps, started approaching. As he walked away one of his heavily tattooed comrades taunted him to stay away from them, but he ignored him and continued to trudge forward.

"He's coming this way." Cody was motioning to stand up, but he felt the missionary put his hand on his arm to halt him.

"Don't be troubled, big man," said the missionary. "That's not the look of malice in his eyes, but of wonder."

The gangster stood right beside the audience and quietly listened in on the message, too much of the silent dismay, however, of not a few of the parents, children, and ministry leaders. Cody happened to glance back when he spotted another group of youths and young men creeping amongst the bottle green palm trees by the first party.

One of the missionaries crossed over by Cody to the gangster, and putting his arm on his shoulder he pointed towards his companions and those creeping out the trees.

When the gangster turned around to look, his face collapsed, and he waved his hands screaming in Spanish for them to look out. The screams proved no avail, however, for before his allies could even hear what he said, the opposing gang ambushed them and opened fire. The cackling of bullets and stark violence didn't seem real at first to the Dark Giant, but he was alarmed enough to stand to his feet. As one of the youths, who was attacked, fell wounded he fired off his gun. Cody then heard the sound of a woman bawling behind him.

"She's been shot," someone yelled.

The horror finally hit him. When he turned he saw the wounded woman fall to the sand holding her leg. All the ministry leaders scrambled to gather all the frightened and screaming children and their parents into the trees for shelter. Compelled by the bravery of his companions, Cody raced to the wounded woman, scooping her into his arms, and hurried her off into the woods with the rest of the assembly.

"The other group's leaving," he heard someone say. As Cody gently laid the woman on the grassy ground he looked back yonder and saw the last of the ambushing party vanish into the fog of trees far away.

"Wait," yelled a voice, "it's not safe to go out there yet!"

Cody then saw the lone gangster who had joined them run of to his ravished friends.

"There might be survivors among the wounded," said Fermin, while motioning with his head for the missionaries to follow him.

"That other gang could still be around," said another ministry leader.

"Then I'll go alone." Fermin hurried off to the wounded lot. One of the missionaries then told another to come with him and both of them ran off to join Fermin, and three more soon followed after them as well.

Cody then looked up from the moaning woman to Catherina. "We've got to get her to a clinic, now."

"Why are they wasting their time checking among those fallen murderers for survivors when we have a true victim of their calamity right here!?" shouted one of the evangelist. As Cody, Catherina and some of the other ministry leaders stared at him in anger he ranted on, "We should leave their filthy corpses for the sand to care for!"

"God shines his light on both the wicked and the righteous, Hector," said another ministry leader. "It is not your place and ABSOLUTELY NOT the time for you to judge them!"

After a few minutes were spent searching for survivors among the wounded, Fermin and the other gangster carried a wounded young man under their arms back to the mission team. As they laid the hurt youth on the grass, Fermin told Catherina, "Go get the utility van."

As the five other missionaries made it back to the mission team, one of the other missionaries standing near Cody asked Fermin, "Were there any other survivors?"

"No, just him," answered Fermin. "The others were only praying with the dying."

Cody then heard the warning sirens of a vehicle backing up. As he stood up a couple of the adults from the neighboring villages waved for their neighbors to make way for Catherina. As one of the evangelists opened up the back doors of the vehicle, Cody, Fermin, and some of the other missionaries carried the wounded woman and gangster into the row less back.

"Go with your daughter to the Managua Baptist Hospital," said an older missionary to Fermin. "We'll get these people back to their homes." He then pointed to Hector, and the other gangster. "You two go with Cody into the van."

Cody and the two men assigned with him hopped into the back of the vehicle, while Fermin leapt into the passenger side.

A few seconds later, Catherina was dashing through roads while the wounded gangster held his stomach in from the now vicious bumps. His remaining comrade was trying to speak softly to comfort him, but the young man managed to mutter out, "Stop saying I'll be okay. Death's waiting for me. I'll go to Hell just like our friends."

Cody glanced up at the wounded youth's friend just to hear what he would say. His mouth was open, but it was choked to a hopelessness hush.

"Hell is where you deserve to go…" said Hector, gently placing his hand on the wounded gangster's shoulder, "…but that is not where you have to go."

As Cody observed Hector share the Gospel to him Cody thought to himself, *Could I be obedient enough to Christ to even witness to the ones hate?*

CHAPTER SIX

That night, while all the missionaries were fast asleep in a large house off the shore of Lake Cocibolca, Cody was awake sitting on the front steps reminiscing of when Hector had preached to the gangster. He was busy rocking back and forth in one of the four rocking chairs on the cement porch, until he came to a slow pause. Taking his enormous, bare webbed feet off the railed legs of the chair, he planted them on the warm rough concrete while hunching forward.

"Jesus," prayed the Dark Giant in a soft voice, "could I witness to Wiebe like Hector did to that gangster?"

He then painted what he could remember of this man in his mind. It had been sixteen years since he'd seen him, and all he could recollect of him was that he was blonde and tall, yet much smaller than him. He imagined trying to share the Gospel with him, but a heat of anger flowed into his body. He smiled hoping forced joy would keep the exercise positive. It didn't. A flash of fire and warped metal breached his mind. What caused that explosion? That slender blonde man did. Vengeance shrouded him. He then remembered when he clasped his hands like a snare around Wiebe's lean long neck ramming him into a wall behind him.

Suddenly, he felt a singe in his heart. He knew it wasn't muscular, and he knew Who it was. "Sorry, Jesus." Straightening up from his trance he looked down at his hands and saw that they were like talons ready to strangle. "I can't even forgive him."

Then, he felt something large and hairy crawling up his arm, and when he turned over his left forearm to investigate, it was what had to be the most hideous gray multi-eyed eight-legged fiend he'd ever seen! Dropping his right hand like a hatchet he smashed it, and quickly shot up shaking its mushy remains to the floor.

He looked around frantically on the steps a few seconds more for any more unwanted spiders. As he slowly sat back down scanning again in every possible direction, he saw Catherina calmly appear in the screen door.

"What's ailing you, Cody?" she asked with a look of concern.

"Nothing's ailing me now. Just can't say the same for that asinine arachnid though." Cody was always irked whenever someone saw him scared, especially a woman; particularly this woman in this case. He tried holding it in, but a little of the heat seethed through his teeth. "What are you still doing up?"

She just snickered as she stepped through the door. "I should ask you the same question."

"Fair enough." He then stared at the half cut pineapple in her hands that she was drinking from. "What's that, your fourth tonic pineapple drink this week?"

"My sixth," answered Catherina with a smile.

"Ha. You got a little gluttony in you, Cat."

"You could say that," she paused smacking her lips, "but pineapples don't grow in Japan." While chopping up the chunks of fruit in the shell, she gave him a look inviting him to take a spoon full. Cody nodded 'yes' and leaned his head over, opening his mouth. As she fed him she continued, "And they're free here."

He was too distracted to enjoy all the notes, but the cool sting of the citrus flesh and sparkling water that it swam in pleased him enough. "That's good," he said, licking his lips.

"I can make you one if you…"

"No, I'm fine," he said with a wave from his hand.

The Dark Giant watched her as she continued chopping the chunks in the half. He felt a cool breeze brush against his cheek. As it grew stronger he noticed it playing with the lovely mantle of Catherina's hair. She paused closing her eyes in what looked like bliss.

"I always loved the nights down here," she said while rising up her long chin.

He was entranced, but this state wasn't filled with the same heated malice like the one before. It was warm and gentle. She then glanced down at him with her pale, slitted hazel eyes. "Something puzzling you, Kodiak?"

Man, he griped to himself, *she's just like mom.*

"You're sour, and those small grey irises aren't really good for keeping secrets."

"Hm." Cody smirked while slowly turning his head away. He remained silent, stopping his eyes on the silver crescent moon slicing into the water ahead. Catherina was indeed much like his mother. He knew she was staring at him with that same calm anticipation his mom had when she was waiting for an answer. He could feel the energy on his neck.

"The Indian in Goma and me is Arapaho," Cody finally answered, "which was what my mom mentioned to you when you two talked about the mission she works at. We grew up knowing who our father's parents were, but we never knew our mother's folks. When we were older she told us that the reason for that was because her father shunned her from the tribe when she showed him that her fiancé, my soon to be father, was a Christian; let alone a black man.

"A couple of years back mom was looking for missions to join at Native American Reservations, but she never had any success. Some point during the failures to get in she realized that the Lord was hindering her because she had never made an attempt to be reconciled with her own father. She felt, 'how can He have me going about preaching that man must be reconciled to their Father if I myself didn't try to be reconciled with my own.' So she took me and Goma to Colorado to see her parents on the rez for the first time. Her mother was able to warm back up to her, but her father avoided us during the whole time we were there. He never apologized for forsaking her, but my mom chose to obey God and forgave him to his face anyway."

"That must have been a powerful moment for you two," said Catherina.

Cody had paused for a couple of seconds as he leaned back in the chair. "Seeing Hector share the Gospel to the very gangsters he hated today reminded me of what God did through momma. I was pretty challenged. So I was just wondering while I was out here if I could obey Him and do the same thing to my father's murderer." Cody then looked back up at Catherina with a frustrated glare. He wagged his head. "Can't do it."

CHAPTER SEVEN

There was now a good silence between the both of them. Cody was hoping the quiet would discomfort Catherina enough to leave, but hearing the wood from the chair scrape the concrete as she dragged it over quickly dashed his hopes.

"Was it intentional?" she asked while putting her pineapple on the ground.

"No," answered Cody. "He spun him out at a high speed. Dad's car got air-born."

There was another quiet passing. Suddenly he felt her hand latch to his arm. When he glanced over to her, her eyes were fixed on his as if she had interpreted an omen.

"Was your father Cody Johnson Senior?"

"Yeah."

"The Johnson, Sr. who died in that awful crash at the 12 of Hours of Nurburing sixteen years ago?"

"Yeah."

"Wiebe Hramn was the man that killed your father?"

"Yeah."

Her grasp then became a rub. "I'm so sorry for you and your family. That was a horrible to see. Must have been devastating?"

"Very." Cody nodded his head while looking away. "Yeah, Momma had to catch Goma before she fell to the floor. Rick, who was my father's engineer at the time, was just standing petrified at dad's burning car on the garage monitor."

"And you?"

He was trying to recall his reaction, but fear stopped him. He felt it would completely discolor his character from before, yet to his surprise she concluded...

"You must have been the one your father's crew and the officials had to haul from Diederick's garage."

"Yeah." He looked her way again, and to his delight he saw no fear in her eyes.

"Would you have killed him?"

"I almost did. If Rick and those boys hadn't got there in time I would have."

A short quiet had again fallen on them.

"Well," said Catherina, "I know that it was God who carried you all through the pain. How did He do it?"

"Well, to be honest He would have been able to heal Goma and me sooner had we not ran away from Him for so many years. It was only about five years ago when we both stopped and made God our priority."

"Well, what made you guys repent?"

Cody didn't wish to go any further. He put all his energy into hiding his angst. He was never really one who enjoyed probing questions, especially ones that infringed the doors of what he considered his most shameful chapter. "It's a long story."

"Well the night's young. I'm willing to listen."

He again restrained his angst and glanced over to Catherina just to determine whether she was questioning for questioning's sake. To his surprise, she had that same look of concern. Much of him wanted to just leave, but the spirit between them was comforting and he knew that him withdrawing wouldn't take that air with him. Besides, in all shallow frankness, to refuse the company of such a woman whose intentions to him seemed completely sincere was simply out of the question.

Where do I start thought Cody. As he began recanting to Catherina he remembered that delicious steak dinner some fellow ANSCA competitors treated him and some of his team mates to at a plush resort named Gata on the main strip in Vegas. He could recall every bite of that seared cayenne and brown-sugared caramelized rib-eye. The smoky yet bitey juices from the meat were good enough on their own, but when he took each tender piece and scooped them into the garlicky mashed potatoes beside them, the ecstasy was near fatal. And what brought such a jovial occasion, you might ask; why they were celebrating Cody's first win as a rookie in ANSCA, as well as what would probably go down as one of the best vindictive victory celebrations in the history of the sport.

"So, how much did the officials fine you for doing that burnout in front of Slim's garage," asked one of the drivers sitting beside Cody.

"Billy," said the Dark Giant nodding his head to his then crew chief, "The big Whigs give us any of the bad news yet?"

"Nope," answered Billy, while taking a gulp of his Bud light. "They probably figure on letting the glitz and glam of tonight buffer up the gloom and doom for tomorrow."

"Fine, or no fine," said another at the table, "that's going down as one of best celebrations ever."

"Yeah, well he had to do something," said another. "Johnson Nation was probably going to tear him apart for not even doing a victory burnout at the stands. Man, you didn't even take a kiss from the SHOW GIRLS.

"That's pride and lust, Gibbs," quipped Cody while taking a sip of his beer.

"Well, I guess all them rubber pullets Slim and his crew are still spitting out of their teeth thanks to you is vice enough to the Big Man upstairs. Serves him right for clipping you into the turf at Richmond, though."

Cody just happened to glance to his left when he noticed a tall dark woman in a grey hoodie sauntering down the hallway. *Raggedy attire, for a place like this* he remembered thinking. As she passed by the massive red lit water fall panels strewn on the beige wall, her chiseled face and violet eyes seemed strikingly familiar. *It can't be. Goma?* He immediately rose from his seat, and went to her. "Goma."

The woman slowed to a halt. He remembered her hand trembling on her purse's strap as he approached her. "What are you doing all the way out here?" He then leaned down to hug her, and pecked her on the cheek.

"Oh, it's just me and some girls on a road trip," she said while adjusting her strap.

When he stepped back to look at her face he saw a grave discomfort. He had always known her to be very quiet with a face as still as an untroubled pond, but her eyes could never truly hide her emotions. He ignored the twinge, however, as his own continence sullened. It had been as almost an unforgivable long time since they last saw each other. He figured his sister must have sensed his guilt because he remembered her squeezing out a smirk saying, "No worries. We knew you had your own life to live."

Feeling the anxiety had finally evaporated between them; he took her by the hand and started walking her back towards his company. He felt some reluctance in her following, but he remembered reckoning at the time that it was just from the weight of her usual bashfulness. "Hey ya'll, I got someone I want ya'll to meet." Cody stopped before everyone while holding his sister by the shoulder. He remembered noticing the agitation on most of the men at the table when he introduced her as his sister. He even recalled Billy choking on his beer.

"Cody," said Goma patting him on the chest, while ducking under his arm. "I've got to go."

Before he could say anything further she hurried off down the hall to the exit door. He then turned around, resting his hands on the black rail that divided the dining area from the corridor, and faced his company. "That was strange." He turned his concerned stare to his crew chief. "You guys wouldn't happen to know what's up with her, would you."

"What are you asking us for?" answered Billy.

One of the drivers wagged his head. "Cody."

The Dark Giant immediately looked his way. "Do you know what she does here…?" The man beside the driver nudged him with his elbow. He then waved his hand. "Never mind, man."

"Hey!" Cody said in a now irritable tone. "Come on, Charlie, spit it out. She does what, here?"

Suddenly one of the other drivers came beside Cody putting his hand on his shoulder. "See that fellow right there?" he said while pointing down the hallway. Cody glanced in the direction the man pointed to and noticed a tall slender figure in a black leather hoodie going through the same door Algoma went through. "That perv's been eyeing your sister like a jackal since you met her in the hallway."

The Dark Giant frowned in fret. Cody then stepped forward while patting him on the shoulder. "Go, get security."

Cody jogged through the exit door, and ran down the stairs. When he finally broke into the parking lot he heard a scream from afar. As he turned in the direction of the yell he saw his sister wrestling with that same man in black. While Cody's legs bolted him to the tumult, the perpetrator tripped Algoma to the ground, swiftly raising a very large knife above his head for a thrust.

"Hey!"

The perpetrator looked up from her only to see the Dark Giant's enormous fist much intent on collision. Cody clocked him clean off of her. The culprit flew hard into the wall on the other side of the violet car she laid by. As two valets stopped in a huff behind his sister, Cody knelt in front of the dark man and grabbed his limp face tilting it left and right seeing if he was still awake. Not getting any reaction except the falling of his thick fake mustache, he went back and helped his sister to her feet.

"Goma." She ignored his call still staring at her attacker. "Algoma." Cody shook her gently.

"What?" she answered as she stared up at him still breathing hard.

"You okay? Did he harm you?"

Algoma's eye's then shriveled in tears as she hugged him burying her face like a drill in his chest. Security finally arrived on the scene trampling towards them. As they pushed the scared valets out of the way; one of them, with his Taser in hand, advanced towards the comatose assailant.

As another of the security guards held his gun on the unconscious culprit, a couple of the guards asked Cody and Goma if they were fine. Cody nodded yes.

"He isn't, though," said the guard feeling about the attacker's wrists and neck. "This creep is dead."

CHAPTER EIGHT

Cody glanced over to Catherina to see if she had found his immense physique in a darker light. To his relief, she only had a look of confusion.

"So that was you guys' turning point?"

"No, no. That's just the background of it."

"Oh," she said, while stroking back her hair, "it just seemed like you had more to say. Did the man know your sister?"

"No." Cody shook his head. "Momma told me the day afterward that his knife's blade matched the stab wounds of six other strippers and burlesque women in Vegas. My sister was his next victim."

"But why would he have been after her."

Cody was silent hoping she would come to the conclusion on her own. Her face finally stirred in subtle shock. "Your sister worked there as a burlesque girl?"

"Yeah."

"Ah, so that's why those men were acting so strange when you brought her to the table."

"Yeah. They probably saw her in an act before I got there."

"Hm." Cody then looked over to Catherina. She seemed to pause in reflection as her waving hair filmed her face. "I forget we were not always saints. Well, God sure did put you at the right place at the right time. So what came afterwards?"

"I left ANSCA and went home."

"Well, I'm sure Goma appreciated the sacrifice you made."

"I wasn't really given an option."

"Yeah, maybe I wouldn't consider it an option either if knew I had to be there to comfort my sister."

"No, I didn't consider it an option because the officials basically forced me out."

"Forced you out? For saving your sister's life?"

"No. They actually called me up to their suite the following morning to give me a check for the time they assumed I was taking off. When I told them I wasn't, the place was in an uproar."

"You were really going to keep racing?" Cody glanced back at Catherina, as she stroked her hair away from her disturbed face. "Why, Cody?"

"I was selfish. All I wanted at the time was to just live my dream. I knew in my heart that the place where God wanted me to be was at home with Goma, but I reasoned that mom would be comfort enough for her."

"So they just suspended you?"

"That's what it was about to come down to. They said it would be irresponsible to let a man, who's still trying to cope with having to kill a man to save a life, race with other people at high speeds. They told me they'd force me to leave for a couple of months if I didn't go on my own. So I quit."

Cody reclined in the chair. He was really hoping to not go any further. As another quiet calm came upon them he figured this would be the end.

"So, what was it like when you finally came home?"

His hope was dashed again! He then hunched forward in his chair and let out a big sigh through his nose.

Cody always used food as a mental road mark when telling accounts, and in this case it was the warm, spicy aroma of his mom's corn, pumpkin-spiced pancakes. He remembered being in a deep sleep from a very disappointing day, and only a smell that hadn't registered in his brain for many years could stir the Dark Giant from his slumber. As he stood, with the dawn's beam on his face, he gave a big yawn stretching wide. Snuggling his feet into his grey supple slippers, he walked out of his room down the hallway rubbing his stomach.

As he neared the kitchen, his mom glanced up at him as she put the glass pitcher of orange juice on the table. "Food never fails," she said with a smile.

He leaned down to hug her while pecking her on the forehead. He then looked at the clock on their large black microwave, and saw that it was 9:33 a.m. "Goma's still a bat when it comes to mornings, huh?"

"Yeah, but this is even a little too late for her," his mother sighed placing a large plate of scrambled eggs on the table. "I better go get her up now, or she won't wake till noon."

A few seconds after she left the kitchen, Cody slowly reached out to the platter of golden orange pancakes, picking up a large crumb from the pile. He remembered how good that crumbly, spicy, sweet melody played on his tongue. He hadn't taste anything like it since he left for the Air Force.

"CODY!!"

The Dark Giant almost choked on his stolen morsel. *Talk about eyes in the back of her...*

"CODY!!"

Believing that was too loud for a warning to not be greedy, he scurried out of the kitchen down the hallway towards his sister's room. "Momma, what's wrong?" he asked as he approached her.

When she turned around, the look on her face made him feel like a wrench clamped onto his intestine. It was the same timorous look she had sixteen years ago when his father died. With trembling hands she handed him a note. When he took the paper he looked over at the envelope left on his sister's well-made bed; "To a Better-off Johnsons." it read. Cody immediately returned his eyes to the letter and opened it;

> Dear Momma and Cody,
>
> The first thing you folks are going to be astounded by is how immaculate my penmanship is. Tidiness was never a virtue for me as you both know. Anyway, I'll keep this short. You saw that I addressed the envelope to a *Better-off Johnsons*. That's because I know that's how you'll be when I'm out of the picture; permanently. Don't be grieved. I'm even going to make sure I disappear where no soul can find me so the news won't remind you all that I existed. I'm sorry Cody for stealing your dreams. I'm sorry momma for being born. God bless you two.

Though it had been five years since he'd read that note he remembered it word for dreadful word. Particularly because he knew that the Lord warned him to not make up his mind to get back into ANSCA, and not to argue with the officials in taking some time off. But he didn't obey Him. He just didn't realize at the time that when Goma would hear on the news that he had quit ANSCA she would blame herself. That coupled with his reluctance to show a good attitude when he finally got home last night, and him abruptly leaving the dinner table when his mom accidentally eluded to something about racing.

But instead of taking any guilt to his head of what Goma did he just frowned and griped, *"God bless you two?"* He balled up the letter. "That little selfish ..."

"Cody!" yelled his mom while trying to pry open his fist. "We can give that note to the police. What on earth's wrong with you?"

He then released the crumpled paper in his mother's hands.

"We need to go to the sheriff's department. God only knows how long she's been gone."

"She couldn't have been for too long. I heard her shufflin' about in her room a little over an hour before I got up."

His mother's eyes shot him with ire dread. "Why didn't you tell me that when you came in the kitchen?!"

"What? How were we supposed to now she was sneaking out of here at the time?" He sighed, while rubbing his head in thought. "Look, I'll go drive around Cotulla and Laredo to see if I can find her. Meantime you check with the police. I'll call you if I find anything."

CHAPTER NINE

Cody remembered those several hours driving to and from Cotulla and Laredo and back being a frantic waste of time. He stopped by all the gas stations, houses and farms showing all the clerks and residents Goma's picture asking if they saw her. Yet, no one could identify her.

A little while later he met up with his mother at the Sherriff's department and they both gathered together at a little wooden table in the facility's tiny kitchen. For a while the two of them just sat together in quiet apprehension. Cody then turned his eyes away from the television above to his mom. "I probably already know the answer to this, but have the police heard any tips to Goma's whereabouts?"

"No." His mom quietly exhaled through her little nose as she leaned forward with her head in her hands. "They're still trying to track down some missing teen. They'd have better luck with that." He was twinged by her drop in tone. It was like a vacuum sucked the weight out her voice.

"You think she's dead don't you?"

"What makes you think she isn't?" He remembered her doe-like brown eyes rolling back up to his, as if all life was raped from them. He knew this wasn't fear, but more of a gradual surrender. "Four hours is a long time to finally muster the nerve to kill yourself."

She dropped her stare to the table resting her hands there as well. "I must have been a bad mother." She nodded in agreement to what she said.

Cody's mouth could have dropped to the table if it was long enough. He then felt a dark presence pass by him. He stared in its direction. He knew what it was.

"That's probably why Smoky's gone, too," she continued. "Could have been a better wife."

Cody looked back to his mom, and the look on her face was so down even the ocean's farthest leagues shied of its plummet. The Devil had dealt her such a blow. It was as if only a warm husk sat before him, instead of his mother. He remembered, at the time, her plea two years into his service at the Air-Force, "I just wish you were here Cody. That girl's becoming such a menace."

The Dark Giant stopped as his eyes moistened. He had again taken the emotions from that memory to stab himself. He raised up his head to the sky messaging his lids. He didn't even look over to Catherina. Out of shear pride, he couldn't. After a sigh through his large bull nose, he continued where he had left off. He remembered leaning towards her, covering his mother's hands with his. "You know the one thing we didn't do before we split up to find her was pray." His mom eyes returned to his. He saw a small light flicker deep within as a stream of hope slid down her face cheek.

"Jesus," he started, while closing his eyes, "God we come to you in prayer today, for Goma. Lord, I know she thinks she's doing mom and me a favor by ending her life, but you know she's not. Please God, if she's still alive, bless that we're able to find her and convince her to not go through with her plans. Send your angels to her to talk her out of giving up. Please soften her heart to repent from her sins and come back home. Please Father. Your will be done. Amen." As Cody opened his eyes he felt the malevolence leave.

"Amen," sniffled his mom as she raised her head.

As Cody happened to glance up at the T.V. above them, he saw a commercial with a car passing by a highway billboard. His little bear-like eyes perked up. *That's it. She's got to be there!* "Thank you, Jesus," he whispered.

"For what, dear?" asked his mother.

"For revealing to me where she is."

An hour and a half later, Cody was charging north in his truck on Interstate 35. As he slowed into the slow lane, surely, as he had hoped, he and his sister's childhood spot appeared a mile away. A few minutes later, he climbed up to the old billboard's platform and saw Algoma sitting on the opposite edge of it. Her back was still towards him as he stopped behind her.

"Hey, Goma," he said.

"Hey Cody." She kept her face forward while slowly kicking her legs back and forth on the edge. "You never were one to get the hint."

"And what *hint* was that?"

"That I don't want to be bothered."

"You didn't expect momma and me to just twiddle our thumbs when you left did you?"

He then glanced over her head and saw a long silver hand gun nestled in her lap. His stomach wrung of itself any pleasantness as distress filled its way in.

"Why isn't momma with you?" His sister leaned over to look down at his Durango. "She ain't in the truck as far as I can see." She then straightened up. "I guess her *unconditional love* for me is finally expired."

"Your momma's *unconditional love* was spent looking for you. I told her to wait at the Sheriff's Department in case I didn't find you. You need to stop this silly charade and come back home."

His sister, however remained silent, and with each soundless second, Cody's irritation grew. "You killing yourself isn't going to bring relief to us, just pain. The same bullet you'll use in your head will go through her heart."

"Oh. Cut the bull, Cody. Momma's already moved on, and you're too slow to catch it. That's why she's not here with you. If she had any inkling of hope in her she'd be here with you and you know it. You're still in denial. You probably just showed up here so YOU could prove to yourself that YOU CARED!"

This stung the Dark Giant. "Wait, you calling me selfish? Selfish, for trying to drag your apathetic hide back home."

"So, you're my knight in shining armor. Gee, well, reality sure did whap me good in the head, because you were never around."

"What do you mean I was never…"

"I left for Vegas four years ago, Cody. That makes it ten years you've been gone. Ten years, Cody, and don't even give me any of that garbage saying you came by when I was gone. If you didn't show your face around the house for the six I was there, you sure didn't show it when I left!"

"You were really gone for ten years?" interjected Catherina, while stroking her hair back.

Cody looked over to her. "Yeah."

"Did you ever visit them?"

He shook his head. "No."

"That's pretty bad Cody." She raised her eyebrows. "How did you become so selfish?"

As Cody continued on, Catherina's question was best answered through his sister's candid, albeit crude words, "You were too busy chasing your LEOTARD – RACING dreams to care about us. While mom was putting up with my drinking and whoring around all you did, at best, was call up and lecture me on how to behave."

One thing he feared about his sister was her stiletto of a tongue. She never wasted words with a barrage hoping to land a blow, but instead focused them into a compact venom making the right wound. He could never remember being a victim of this weapon, until that day. He then remembered scrambling up the little armor he had left saying, "Hey, I had my own life to live, remember."

"Ha, ha, some life it was. It crashed and burned when you killed that stalker."

His blood became hot in a flash. He glowered at her. "Your faith in that *loser* God of yours is more potent than mom's to try to save the girl that RUINED your career."

"I SAVED YOUR LIFE YOU CALLOUSED WRETCH!"

"You would have saved my life a long time ago if you had killed our father's murderer."

"What?!"

"Maybe if you would have finished killing him, like a good son should have, I would have felt better about myself knowing that my father's murderer was dead and buried. Maybe I wouldn't have had to drown my grief with stripping, men, and booze."

Cody's swelled fists of restraint morphed into ready weapons of harm. He even heard voices, who he, at the time, believed were all his own urging him to follow through with his malicious thoughts. But he just closed his eyes while lifting his head to the sky trying to breathe out the fury within.

"Why don't you make yourself a real hero and kill me like you did my perpetrator."

He then remembered at that time an old cold feeling he had leaking into his heart. It was old because he remembered it first came when he saw Wiebe driving back to his garage after he had killed his father. The other voices, as well as his own intensified their goading. Suddenly, he felt the Spirit burning in him to repent. Giving a huge exhale with his eyes closed he whispered to the Lord. "I'm sorry, Jesus. Please forgive me for my thoughts. Only you can change hearts, not me. Please, please guide me in what you would have me say to her."

He then remembered a calm coming over him, and he became aware of the same malevolent presence he felt when he was with his mom. *Demons.* He scowled hard in disgust, looking around as righteous anger ignited within him. At that moment, he realized whose those other voices were. He was about to motion with his lips to rebuke them, but the Lord moved in him not to. He then felt Him urging him to focus back on his sister. He obeyed.

Cody then slowly slouched behind her.

"You're better off leaving, Kodiak. I'm locked in gear for what needs to be done."

"Then why haven't you pulled the trigger yet?" His sister's back was still towards him, but he heard nothing from her mouth. "Because you don't have a clue where you'll end up when the bullet pops through your skull."

"Oh, don't come at me with that Heaven and Hell garbage."

"If you're so certain that *garbage* doesn't exist then why haven't you pulled the trigger?"

"Because..." His sister sighed in irritation.

"*Because* pulling that trigger is not going to fulfill the hope of ending your pain, it's just going to end you."

"We all go to darkness and nothing when we die anyway, Cody. There's no *brilliant light* or *fiery furnace*."

"Our father didn't believe that, Goma, and you don't either. Every man's soul longs for eternity. You have that longing because your soul does last forever, but where it rests is up to you..."

"Alright, I've had it." His sister grabbed the pistol from her lap, and cocked the hammer back. "I'd rather end it now than to discuss religion." She aimed the barrel at her temple while turning around rising to her feet. As Cody stepped towards her she pointed the gun at him. "And if you try to be heroic again, I won't be leaving this world alone."

He remembered not fearing the barrel being pointed to him, but he did feel the Spirit restraining him.

"Now just leave me here. I don't want you around."

"I can't stop you. But you can't make me leave, either."

"Fine," she shrugged, and raised the gun back to her head. "You'll just be in for a messy show."

Cody felt the Holy Spirit's power surge in him. When he opened his mouth it felt like a cold spring was going to gush out. "Just one more thing you should reckon before you take your *Vicodin* to messy bliss, GOMA." He had never felt such force come through his throat. He was stunned at what he was doing, or about who was really doing it, but he was compelled by the Holy Spirit to continue to say what He wanted him to say. "There's is no rest for the wicked. You drop that mallet now in the state you're in and God will reward you with eternal agony, not peace. He will condemn you to the very place our father chose at one point in his life to avoid; the place where everyone deserves to go. AND THERE IS NO ESCAPE."

His sister's finger shivered on the trigger as streams flowed down her cheeks. He stood in suspense as she closed her eyes. He even moved his hand slightly from his side, hoping he could snatch the gun from her. The Spirit, however, moved him not to. The quiet that followed was unsettling. He remembered feeling the trepidation emerging from his sister, yet feeling even more of the immense warmth of the Lord's presence around them.

Algoma burped out a scream as her eyes sprung open, and she flung the gun away from her to the ground below.

CHAPTER TEN

Algoma then held her hands over her closed mouth in horror as another moment of eerie quiet passed. Then Cody remembered her doing the most logical thing a person who had just changed their mind from forgoing suicide would do; laugh. Yes, laugh.

"Laugh?" interrupted Catherina

"Yep," said Cody with a nod, "she laughed."

"How could she find humor at such a morbid time?"

"Well, when I asked her what was so funny she said, '"I'm gonna end up in that place sooner or later."'

"What place?" he remembered asking her.

"When my eyes were closed, I saw a vision of a smoldering lake of fire. Lots of souls were just scorching, screaming, tearing. The sheer vacuum of heat robbed my breath. And then I heard God say what you said, but with a, you know, more infinitely authoritative tone, "And there is no escape."

"Is that where you want to go?"

He then remembered her being mute, leaving her new tears to do the speaking. She then looked back up at him with subtle fear, and choked out. "No."

"Then you know what you need to do."

His sister looked down while nodding.

"You've got to leave your life of sin and surrender your heart to Christ. Put your faith in Him and what He did for you on the cross and His resurrection, and He'll forgive your sins."

"But I don't know how long He'll put up with me. I mean, even God's got a limit, right?"

"Nope. Jesus said that whomever the Father gives Him; no one can snatch them out of His hand. He died once and for all to pay for all the sins you've done, all the sins you're doing, and all the sins you'll do in the future. And He will put in you His Holy Spirit to move you to live life the way Jesus lived. In Heaven, there is no eviction."

His sister chuckled at his words. She was again silent for a time. "Would God mind if I had support from someone in doing this?"

"No, He wouldn't, but you have to be the one doing the talking."

"I know, Cody." She then slowly held out her hands to him, and he walked towards her grabbing hold of them. She bowed her head in prayer and verbally trusted her life to Christ.

"When we came back to the Sheriff's Office," said Cody, "momma didn't even wait for us to get through the doors. Soon as she saw us through the glass she ran on through the doors and squeezed Goma like a wish she wouldn't surrender."

Hearing what he thought was sniffling; he glanced over to Catherina and saw her wiping her eyes with her hands.

"Oh, don't mind me," said Catherina with a fling from her hand. "I always get choked up hearing when God miraculously makes good of such bad situations." She then turned her eyes to him stroking away her hair. "And you were the instrument He used to do it."

Cody felt the urge to smile, but the excessive guilt he suddenly conjured strangled it away. He then lowered his eyes to the floor in shame.

"Really, Cody?" This was the first time the Dark Giant had ever heard what sounded like disappointment in her voice. He looked up just to see what it might look like. Her eyes were so squinted by the lowering of her thick eyebrows that they looked more like long thin cracks with only a glitter of light reflecting from within. "What's wrong now? You know, you can be a real downer. I've never seen you like this."

"Cat, none of that wouldn't have happened in the first place if I would have just obeyed God and stayed home all those years."

"But such is life, Cody. At some point, all of us have chosen to disobey God, and then regretted it when we reaped the consequences. But we have to celebrate the victories, too. You ultimately obeyed Him in the end, and look at the miracle that God brought through it."

The Dark Giant still kept a shamed composure. He could still see the disenchantment in her eyes, for she knew he had blocked out all of her words from getting through. You see Cody believed shame, or guilt as he would call it, was a means to keep him "humble". In other words, if any one praised him about anything good that he did, he always reminded himself of the wrong he'd done, particular the transgressions he committed during this time of his life, to stop him from being overly happy or "too proud".

"Okay," said Catherina as she folded her arms reclining back in her chair. "So what happened with your family after you led your sister to Christ."

"Well, Goma and momma got closer. A lot closer. Closer than they were even before I left for Shepherd. Goma went to Cosmetology school and got a job as a hair dresser. She went to church, back in Cotulla, with me and momma every Sunday before she moved out on her own to Laredo. She's been in her Word ever since. She dates, but she's been celibate all these years as far as I know. And you already know about mom."

"Yeah," said Catherina with a nod. "So what about you? Tell me the good stuff first, though."

Cody gave a funny puff through his nose, but when he returned his stare to her there was no trace of humor. He shrugged his shoulders while looking away again. "Well, during that time God showed me my calling to be an evangelist."

"How's that?"

"Well, He really brought that to my attention through some of my church peeps when they saw me witness, in Spanish, to a little old Ecuadorian woman at our food pantry. They told me I should talk with our Evangelism leader, and when I did she offered for me to join her with the Open Air Campaign branch in our state. Since the church and Open Air were basically my full time job I spent a lot of my free time discipling people, doing Bible studies, working out with folks at the gym. I was pretty content with how things were going until I got back into racing with Rick."

"So, you weren't racing before La Sarthe?"

"No. God took that out of my life for a good season."

"Oh." She stroked back her hair while leaning forward. With a dead-pan look she asked, "So how did Jesus ride this big bucking bronco into submission this time?"

"Ha." He smirked while lounging in the chair. His eyes returned back to the lake. He stared on as if using the blue splatter of the sickled moon's reflection to ripple back in time.

CHAPTER ELEVEN

Cody did not use food as a usual landmark to begin his recanting this time, but a verse he had read during a Bible devotion one Saturday morning, "Every branch in me that does not bear fruit he takes away, and every branch that does bear fruit he prunes". *Prune.* He remembered the echo bringing him to a pause. Out of the thousands of times the Dark Giant had read this passage, it was this thousandth and first that caught his attention. *What does 'prune' mean?* He then got up and grabbed the dusty dictionary from his bookshelf and flipped through the pages for the word.

"To cut off or remove dead or living parts or branches of (a plant, for example) to improve shape or growth". He then went back to the Scripture squinting as he read over the passage again in full this time, "that it may bear more fruit."

That it may bear more fruit? He remembered rubbing his chin in meditation. Any time he read a passage that intrigued him he would always take the time to ponder if it applied to him. After a moment of mental excavation, racing seemed to be the only thing he could think of. *Maybe He's cutting this out of my life.* He knew his conscience had had much validity for its case; for the several weeks following his sister's conversion he spent hours on the internet and on the phone looking for any amateur racing events to compete in throughout the country. He seldom ate with his family, and the few breaks he would take from searching for events or watching racing news was to go to church, the gym, and the occasional Bible devotion.

The bronze strings of his heart began to tug him away from reason, as he shook his head. "This can't be." He then got up from his bed with his Bible in hand and headed out of the room and down the hall.

When he popped through the front screen door, Cody turned to his right and saw his mother rocking in one of the gray rocking chairs on the porch. "Hey, Momma, you've probably crossed this passage a couple of times." As his mom looked up, he handed her the Scriptures with his finger pointing to John 13:2. "What does prune mean in that passage?"

"I figured you've been in the Word long enough to know what this text means." This was an old habit Cody had developed since he was child. Any time he'd stumble on a passage he knew conflicted with his thinking, he'd always bring it to his mom hoping she'd give him the meaning he was hoping to hear. He reasoned that if a Saint as wise as her had the same interpretation as he, even if it was flawed, it would get him off the hook as far as accountability to God goes. One would wonder why a routine such as this would have not been put to pasture sooner when he was still young, because it never worked. In fact, he would swear she knew exactly what he was doing because she always gave him back his Bible with a smile saying so, though she never admitted it. Yet he remembered, figuring at the time, that ten years should have dulled her astuteness.

"Look at the context," said his mother as she pointed. Cody then glanced over to see the text her finger was on. "Jesus is the vine, and God the Father is the vine dresser," she continued. "We believers are His branches. He cuts off, or prunes bad parts from our branches in means to make room for good fruit, good works."

Cody nodded his head in agreement as his mother stared him. Her astuteness was still sharp. Sharper than ever, perhaps. But she didn't hand him back the Book with a clever grin as usual. She was still staring at him, in fact, with that "infamous" silent anticipation.

What more does she want he remembered thinking. He turned his attention to the deer grazing the knee high green pasture ahead.

"Something bothering you, Cody?"

"Hm?" He heard her question, pretending his mind was elsewhere.

"Do you feel God's pruning something out of your life to produce good works?"

This he couldn't ignore. He slowly turned his eyes to his mom's and rested them there for a while. "Maybe."

"You think it might be racing?"

Racing? It took nearly all his energy to keep his eyes in their sockets. *Her too?* Her probing was too deep to withstand, and he knew keeping quiet wouldn't halt her yearning for an answer. "I need to finish my reading." He then took back his Bible and went back into the house.

After several more weeks of persistence, he finally stumbled upon an open event in Nevada. As he headed out the door, with bags packed for the trip, he stopped before his family who were waiting on the front porch to see him off.

"Take care, Possum," said Cody as he headed over to his sister.

"Take care, Butterbomb," He then kissed her on the forehead and hugged her, but when he headed over to his mother her air was much colder. He remembered seeing that same blank stare of disappointment she had when he left for Shepherd. He just rolled his eyes, however leaning down to give her a big hug. He was certain this time it would be different.

Several hours later, Cody was thundering down through Route 66 as fast as he legally could. "Good timing." He remembered saying to himself as the "Welcome to New Mexico" sign flew past him. For miles ahead he could only see asphalt and desert. He remembered glancing at his police monitor above his dashboard. "Ah, no Fuzz." With a roguish grin he slowly pressed down on the throttle while up shifting. Cactuses and bushels of grass swooshed by as his speedometer climbed well over 150 mph. He was just about to hit 161 when he saw an armadillo crossing the road several yards ahead. He softly braked swerving out of the knocked out way, while unconsciously up shifting. He glanced up in the rear view mirror in disgust. "Dumb vermin." Like a reflex, with his foot still on the throttle, he down shifted.

Suddenly something like the sound of a truck smashing into a brick wall thumped his ears and chest. "Oh no." Cody looked down at the hood and saw white smoke fuming out from it. "Blast it, man. You missed shift." He dropped the gear all the way to first while crawling his shattered azure and white chariot unto the golden pebble and dirt turf.

He then stepped out of the car, trudging on the gravel to the front of the hood; actually, the gravel might as well have been boot high snow, traveling as slow as he was. He thought a much delayed inspection would lighten the car's severe condition, yet the closer he got to the fumes he wagged his head gripping the grim reality. The Dark Giant popped open the hood and backed off waving the hot smoke from his face. As it cleared, he realized it was much worse than he thought. He then grabbed the red extinguisher from the glove department and frosted the engine. "Blast it."

He slung the empty canister to the dirt. "That, dumb armadillo…" Cody then looked up to sky extending his open arms to God. "Why couldn't you stop the little scum from even getting on the road?!" Anger began to brew in him, but he felt too ashamed to say anything more. His anger, however, turned to bitterness, and he started to feel the Spirit stirring within. *Why is He upset now? He wasn't angry with the stuff I said before.*

Cody could not contain his feelings any longer, and giving into them his tongue threw darts at the Lord. The Spirit's anger intensified as he went on and on pacing back and forth, but he wouldn't relent feeling at the time he had the "right" to let Him have it. "I brought my sister into saving faith with you. I gave up ANSCA for you. What more do you want from me!? You let me down, just like you let my dad..."

Cody gripped his chest as if trying to contain an explosion. His knees started to buckle from the immense ire the Spirit had towards him. "God, I..." The Lord's anger intensified. The sensation he felt was like a volcano about to erupt within, yet his body felt perfectly intact. Too dread-bound to even think another thought, he just plopped in his car. For hours he was petrified on that seat believing that one more careless letter, or imagination would be his last.

CHAPTER TWELVE

For the couple of days following that wreck in New Mexico, Cody neither prayed to the Lord, nor got in his Bible because every time he tried to apologize to Him, or read the Scriptures he felt nothing. One evening Cody was moping in the rocking chair on the front porch watching the sun diminish into the purple and orange horizon. Suddenly, his mother emerged through the door and sat beside him in the other chair.

"Still mourning the loss of Veronica, Kodiak?"

"Whose Veronica?" asked Catherina.

Cody smiled as he gently rocked back and forth in his chair. "My first love."

"First love? I thought that was Paquita. Well, at least that's what you told us over dinner when we first got here."

"No, no Paquita was just my old high school crush. She transferred to another school before I even got a chance to know her. No, Veronica was my 2002 Dodge Viper GTS-R."

"Oh. I see."

Cody then glanced over to Catherina. His smile was now a smirk.

She then rested an elbow on the arm of her chair while nestling her head on her hand. She smiled as her eyes glittered from the light of the moon. "So, why Veronica?"

"Ha." The Dark Giant shook his head. God did him a favor by making him so dark, because if he was any lighter, even a beet would have been made out for a cauliflower. "Veronica, was one of the love interest of Archie. It was a comic book series Daddy used to get for me back in the day. I guess I always had a thing for pale-skinned brunettes."

Catherina giggled as her complexion was tinctured to what Cody's couldn't.

"Daddy won that car for me at a Barret Jackson auction in Houston for my 16th birthday." He paused, almost lifting his head to stop any tears from falling.

"It was a relic of your father."

"Yeah." He nodded his head.

He then continued where he left off. He remembered not saying anything for a while when his mom asked him about his late car.

"Momma," he said, while keeping his eyes fixed ahead.

"Mmhm?"

"Can you drive the Holy Spirit away?"

"No. What makes you feel like He left you?"

He reclined far back in his chair till his buzzed head touched the wooden wall behind. "Back there in New

Mexico, I was pretty angry with the Big Man upstairs after the wreck, you know? I said some heated things I wish I could take back. Hasn't been the same between Him and me ever since. I don't feel His joy, I don't feel His anger; just nothing. Feels like he left me, that's all." He then glanced over at his mom. "That ever happen to you?"

His mom nodded her head with a grin. "Yeah, I have. It was a few years after Smoky was killed. Goma was still raising all kinds of hell while you were gone wrestling. It felt like I was all alone. So in my anger, I told God that He had abandoned me, and boy did I feel His anger. I was too afraid to say another word, and for a day it felt like He wasn't there. I apologized to Him, I even condemned myself, and I did everything I could to get some feeling from Him. It was only until I truly realized *what* sin I committed and confessed it to Him with a true desire to repent from it, that His presence in me felt strong again."

"But you see, that's my point." Cody slowly leaned forward while resting his elbows on his thighs. "Aren't we supposed to lay our hearts bare before the Lord, like the Psalmists do; like Job did?"

"Well, yeah honey, God does tell us to be transparent to Him. He wants us to tell Him how we feel about things, but He won't tolerate us using our emotions as bullets to attack His character. That's the mistake Job made; that's the same mistake I made."

Cody sighed while turning his eyes back to the sunset. He then felt her hand grasp his forearm. "Come.

Let's eat." She then stood up from her chair. "Bar-be-que pulled beef spaghetti, pumpkin corn-bread, and some collard greens. That sounds about good right now, huh Cody?"

The Dark Giant never was much for saying no to culinary temptations. Seconds after his mother rang the verbal dinner bell, he rose from his chair following in after her.

While Cody, his mother, and his sister were all at the kitchen table eating, he remembered Algoma telling everyone about the usual shenanigans at work.

There she goes with those silly stories from the salon again, he thought while chewing.

"SHE WOULDN'T BE HERE TO TELL THEM IF YOU WERE'NT THERE THAT NIGHT TO SAVE HER."

He was terrified, his food nearly hanging out his mouth. He knew Who that still small voice belonged to. He used his fear as fuel to stimulate his mind, reflecting deep on what He said. IF YOU'WERE'NT THERE THAT NIGHT TO SAVE HER....'

"Vegas?" he whispered as he gazed at his sister. The Dark Giant's eyes began to dampen as he went back to the night she almost died. His expression, however, fell to a subtle frown. *Yeah, she should be grateful. Her lifestyle cost me my*...Cody immediately felt the Spirit spark in discomfort within. *Ah man*. Remembering his incident with Him in New Mexico he didn't think any further. He glanced back up at

Algoma while she was still talking. He was about to return his attention to his plate, when the Spirit moved in him to keep it on her. He obeyed.

His sister leaned to their mother in a gesture of sort of humorous discretion. "Kodiak's not going to want to pick me up from work anymore, mom."

"Hm," grunted Cody.

"Why's that?" asked Nadie.

"Well, the girls were always so awestruck with him from day one. Ever since he's been dropping me off for work, they've been telling me he looks familiar. So I finally *spilled the beans.*"

Cody wagged his head. "Possum if you told them who I was…"

"You didn't," said their mother, clasping her hands on her cheeks. "You didn't tell them he was Butterbomb from E.I.W., did you?"

"Hey, someone was eventually going to exploit him of his televised spandexed vocation sooner or later. Why not yours truly? We about almost called the paramedics for one client when her recollection kicked in. She laughed straight for almost half an hour."

Cody smirked while sighing in embarrassment. *Ah, Goma.* He glanced back up at his mother and sister. It had been a long season since he'd seen their beloved chemistry. *We haven't had times like this too often.* His face became puzzled, contemplating why 'this' was so.

"You were too busy chasing your LEOTARD and RACING dreams to care about us." Algoma's spiteful echoes rang in his head. There was truth to those words.

He remembered his eyes watering at that moment when he traveled back to all the times his mother almost pleaded with him to not go to Shepherd. He traveled back to her distaste of him choosing to join the wrestling league where he'd be away from home for another two years. "The six years prior to the four I've spent in Vegas you never once showed your face around the house. Ten years, Cody!" Cody buried his head in his hands trying to hide the liquid flood that gushed.

The water from his eyes now began to breach the dam of his fingers, as he remembered what his mom always repeated to him on the phone before Goma left for Vegas, "I wish you were here Cody. She's always looked up to you."

Cody shot up from his seat with futile attempts of drying his eyes.

"Honey?" said his mom.

Cody, still looking down, waved his hand. "I'm fine, I'm fine."

The Dark Giant strode down the hall to his room. Closing the door behind, he couldn't even make it to his bed, his grief bringing him to his knees. He cried out to the Lord from the true agony of his heart. He remembered being doubled over with his face pressed into the brown wooden floor. Through the Spirit's encouragement he confessed all his sin before the Lord in full vigor, splashing the flooded floor with his hand as he wept. "I've been so selfish, Jesus! All these years I only sought the desires of my own heart! I didn't care about you or anyone else!" It was not a short moment that Cody spent on his knees. He felt God's presence stronger in him. Stronger than even when his father was alive.

Feeling he had said all he could say he rose from the floor. He then remembered looking up and noticing his ANSCA poster on the ceiling. He scowled as he reached up and tore down the poster. Balling it up, he noticed all the other trophies for racing, wrestling, and weight lifting that sat on the dressers and shelves of his room, and in his new found zeal he grabbed all of them piling those into his barrel-sized trash can.

Cody passed down the hallway with his trash barrel in arm. He saw the concerned stares his mother and sister gave him as he went by, but paid them no mind. As the front porch light flicked on he grabbed the metal garbage can by the steps, and walked towards the garage. He then lifted up the garage door, and when the light came on he saw the blue tarp covering the corpse of his Viper. He remembered his emotions tugging hard at his soul. Memories of his father flooded in fast of the day he won him that car. He looked down at the trophies that punctured through the poster in the barrel he brought from his room, and reminisced of when his father was there to cheer him on when he was racing go-carts as a child. He remembered the rush of going fast, the tension of going wheel to wheel to get the edge, the thunders cracked from pedigree engines, the sense of gratification in winning. *Is racing altogether bad?* Cody immediately felt troubled, but he remembered that at that moment he never felt the singe of the Lord's scorn. In fact he didn't even feel God's encouragement to do what he had intended to go through with the contents.

"I guess the decision's up to me." He frowned while nodding his head. "I want you Lord. Racing and everything else has to go, permanently." He grabbed the lighter fuel from the bottom cabinet of their grill, and dumped all the articles out of his barrel into the metal can. After he brought the can to the gravel part of the driveway, he put it down and sprayed the stuff inside with the fuel. With the fire starter lit, Cody looked up to God. "To repentance, Jesus." He then lowered the starter to the barrel lighting the poster on fire, and stood back watching the remnants of his past burn.

CHAPTER THIRTEEN

"I'm so grateful for Him letting me even see a race again." Cody shook his head sponging as much shame as he could from this dismal time. "Those final minutes we had before we took our places on the grid at La Sarthe, I just got sort of worked up looking around at the people cheering, the engines starting, the smell of diesel and gasoline; man, I was almost brought to tears. I'm not worthy."

He glanced over at Catherina hoping she was moved by the bearing of his pain. She was moved indeed, but to his surprise the direction appeared to be in exasperation. Her oval face now was more like a falling dagger, while her glittering eyes were so fixed on his they seemed to grasp his soul.

"I know now what's bothering you, Cody," said Catherina.

"What's that?"

"You feel bad when you get things wrong?"

"Yeah."

"Why?"

"Well, everyone wants to get things right, right? No one likes to fail."

"Did you fail when you joined the Air Force?"

"I'd say so. Yeah."

"Did you fail when you went into wrestling?"

"Yeah."

"Was it a failure when you went into ANSCA?"

"Yeah." He shrugged. With each second, he was becoming more irked from her stare. He straightened his posture, clasping his hands, hoping to show he wasn't afraid.

"Why were those failures?"

Cody almost rocked his head back. To him the question seemed too absurd to come from her. "You've been here listening the whole time. You mean you don't…"

Her eyes didn't waver, and out of fear of what she'd do if he refused to comply he answered, "I didn't obey Him, that's why. So what's your prognosis?"

"That's it right there. You don't obey God."

"What do you mean I don't obey Him?"

"Why haven't you obeyed your Father, by forgiving Wiebe?"

Cody looked down as if franticly trying to grasp answers from the cement. He thought he felt vulnerable before when he shared about his past. He just couldn't make sense of how disobedience was now the possible issue. "I'm just not ready for that now."

"Why?"

"Somethings are just a process."

"Meaning?"

He felt like he was being skewered to a wall with a pitch fork, and every effort he made to squirm free just seemed to get him more and more pinned. "I just don't want to now." He failed to withhold some of the fire within from his words, but when he looked back up she had that same piercing stare. A little part of him said that since he was built like a bear he might as well make out like one to deliver him from this "wretched" soul surgery. But the major part of him was too trepid to move. Catherina was barely five feet in height, but she appeared to have no fear of him at all, and it seemed like she really possessed the might to end him if necessary. Stranger still, she didn't seem to realize it, nor did she appear to take any comfort in his discomfort; she didn't even let out a sneer. Her attention seemed completely focused on him. *I wonder if this is God through her.* The thought sparked a knot in his belly. A subtle defiance began to surge.

"I mean, what do I have to prove that I've been obedient?"

"What do you mean by, 'what do I have to prove'?"

"Look, I've been getting in my Word night and day. I've been going to church non-stop now for five years. I gave up racing for Him because it was in the way between us. I've been doing Evangelism full time for three years. I'm here on this mission trip in the middle of nowhere with you, right?"

"So these past acts of obedience equate you from obeying God in forgiving?"

Cody sighed through his nose.

"Do you rejoice in your failures?"

He frowned. The "noose" on his soul tightened hard enough that all armor, even the armor he may have imagined was there was crushed. *You can't be telling me that's a sin, God.* No restraint left to hide the anger, he raised his eyes to Catherina and hissed, "It is how I stay humble."

Catherina, again flinchless replied, "So reminding yourself of when you failed keeps you humble?"

"Yeah."

"Being humble means not thinking yourself higher than you are right?"

"Yeah, that's right."

"And for the context of a believer that means believing God is higher than you?"

"Yeah."

"Doesn't Christ say through Paul that in Him there is no condemnation?"

"Yeah. 'He stands with the Father to intercede for us. Who can come against us?'"

"Then how is reminding yourself of your failures making you humble?"

The air was still quite soupy, but it did little to warm the frigid wind that now breached the Dark Giant's heart. The light in his eyes was all but gone, as blank as a paper.

"Wouldn't condemning yourself, in and of itself be considered disobedience?"

Cody slumped as if succumbing the pulling of an anvil chained around his neck. He hadn't felt this scared or exposed since he was eleven when his dad found out he broke his own bedroom window. He heard wood scraping against cement thinking Catherina was scooting her chair closer, but he didn't bother to look up.

"What was one of the reasons Jesus obeyed God, even to the crucifixion?" she asked as her chair stopped.

Cody was too down to really give a reply. He just couldn't get over that his "secret weapon" to keep him "on track" with the Lord was really legalistic rebellion. He was so into himself that Catherina's phonemes sounded more like fuzzy tic-tacs emptied into his lobes. The only words he could make out were 'reasons', 'Jesus' and 'crucified'.

"He loved Him?" he answered.

"Yes," said Catherina, "that's why. Remember what He said, "If you love me, you'll obey my commandments."

He then felt two very soft hands grasp his.

"Do you love him?" asked Catherina.

Cody frowned, believing his integrity was under attack. *I think I know now how Peter felt.* Thinking of the

Apostle he remembered him denying Jesus three times. *But, I do love You.* Feeling Catherina was definitely sort of God's arbiter before him, the urge to prove himself gave him the confidence he needed to look her in the eyes. "But isn't what I'm doing here obedience to Him? The whole reason we're down here is to spread His Word."

"So loving God in the past builds you up enough heavenly credit to not love Him, now?"

Cody fell his brows in confusion.

"Condemning yourself only reminds you of the person you put to death when you got saved. If you keep reminding yourself of your failures, you'll just feel comfortable failing to obey Him again. Remember what God said through Paul, 'One thing I do, forgetting what's behind and pressing on towards the mark.' You've got to keep your eyes on Him through obedience, Cody, not on you. That old man ran away from God for ten years and almost lost his family because of it, but when that new man obeyed he got his family back, and racing."

Cody felt her grip tighten with these words. "Free yourself from you, Cody. Obey the Master."

Free yourself from you. With these words the Spirit woke the Dark Giant up. *I guess my self-pity really is a choice.* He had been looking Catherina in the eye the whole time, but newly found alertness lifted what seemed like a fog from his eyes. For the first time, he realized her face was drenched. He actually wondered who she was crying for.

"Okay, he said with a smirk.

Catherina wiped her eyes with a sniffle. Returning her hand to his, she nodded with a smile. With that they both bowed their heads and prayed.

CHAPTER FOURTEEN

As Cody was evangelizing with Catherina and her family down in Central America, the president of Diederick Motor Sports Division was briskly walking towards his office in his facility located on the plains of Frasia, Germany.

"Mr. Eggert," said his secretary as he was about to open his door, "you have a visitor."

"And what stray have you let in this time, Olga?" said the president with an annoyed tone as he stopped. "Time after time I have told you; I do not have anyone up here during this..."

"He insisted sir."

"Who insisted?"

His secretary then looked up at him through the slim golden rims of her glasses. "Wiebe Hramn."

Mr. Eggert pouted deep and doubtful. "Wiebe Hramn?" he said to himself. He then opened the door and walked in, seeing his old tall and slender employee holding up the wall to his left. "Well, if it isn't die Schlange, in the flesh, or scales rather," said the president as he turned to face him with his arms folded. "And what brings me the pleasure of seeing you slither back into my chambers?"

Wiebe straightened himself up from his hunch with his hands shoveled in the pockets of his gray slacks. He then stared at him with his cold pale blue eyes. "When does training start for next year?"

The president snickered until it elevated to all out laughter. He then walked away as his diaphragm continued to trumpet notes of hilarity, plopping hard in the chair behind his desk. "You, Mr. Hramn?" he said as he slowly spun around to face him, "A sense of humor actually lurks within that cadaver?"

His guest however watched him with no signs of comedy.

"You're really serious aren't you? Well, in case you haven't noticed, we've moved on from the near two years you've been gone."

"And have your new drivers brought Diederick any titles in my absence?"

"Winning isn't everything Mr. Hramn. And Diederick is not so desperate for acclaim to acquire again the dastardly services from a pariah like you."

"Only fools race to lose." Mr. Eggert stood up out of his chair like a mad badger, yet Wiebe continued, "Diederick found good use of *this* pariah's *dastardly* services for the thirteen years he gave it; and twelve titles to show for it."

"You have the nerve to come in this office and insult me and this establishment…" The president threw up his hands while looking down in bewilderment. "Why am I even talking with you?"

"I win, that's why you're talking to me. I win, and one who wins makes a great asset for a rival manufacturer."

"Rival manufacturer?" Mr. Eggert rolled his eyes. "And what is this fool *rival* you speak of; Raffinato?"

"Twelve titles detours most prejudices. Victory beats manners."

The president receded with a subtle look of vulnerability. The silence of compromise had gushed into the room, and Wiebe was the unwanted vulture it blew in.

"When do I start training for next year?"

"Well that's just fantastic," said a tall regal middle-aged man while standing amongst his party of friends and some of his administrative staff at a golf course. He then glared at his secretary. "Your humor pure sadism."

"I, I," stammered his secretary, "I would've kept it secret until the Futuro Della Velocità Rally in February…"

"No, no your timing couldn't be any better. That gives us ample time to stop World War 3." He then turned to his vice president and said, "Tell Diederick that Wiebe is out, and that…"

"That can't happen, Laurent," said the vice president.

"What do you mean 'can't happen'? Why?"

"Your pretense for expelling him from the sport would seem prejudicial at best. You have no legal grounds to keep him from participating next year."

"What's legal about a murdering hostile racer being permitted to run loose on the track?"

"All those transgressions were not deemed severe enough for I.N. to bar him from racing at the time."

The president pressed his forearm on his club's grip while squinting his livid eyes as he listened on.

"President Meinrad, being the biased German he was, saw Wiebe as the future of I.N. racing. He excused Johnson Sr.'s tragedy to be due to a young man's inexperience and rambunctiousness. Diederick was disqualified of the title and Wiebe was reprimanded with four months of driving behavior classes, a six month ban from any league sponsored by I.N., and was required to take sessions with a psychiatrist. He and Diederick complied with those demands. At the time, as far as the brass was concerned, it was sufficient."

"Sufficient." The President then stroked back his salt and peppered hair as dsimay filled his light brown eyes.

"Why all this fuss about this Wiebe character?" asked one of his friends.

"Because the son of the man Wiebe murdered is racing in the International Nurburgring THIS SEASON!! Animosity at over 300 miles is a CARNAGE waiting to happen!" Laurent stroked his head again while closing his eyes in short deliberation. "We'll just have to terminate this year's Tier One class."

Some of the officials grumbled amongst each other.

"That would be the end of the I.N. as we know it," said the vice president.

"Why's that!?"

"First of all, a lot of manufacturers invested a lot of time and resources in their prototype curriculums. You cancel the tier and the manufacturers will have our throats. Not to mention the outcry the media will have for us eighty-sixing our main attraction. Laurent, manufacturers would rather tolerate racing with a reckless one-time murderer for thirteen more years, then to not race at all."

Laurent chopped his club like an axe into the turf. Leaping the crowd almost out of their shoes. The President then gave a heavy sigh as he squatted to the ground before his iron.

CHAPTER FIFTEEN

It was only a few weeks after his trip to Central America that Cody had to mobilize his team to make it to Monaco for the premier of the Futuro Della Velocità, Italian for "Future of Velocity". During the Thursday afternoon before the International Nurburgring season would kick off, the league's Tier One cars were being led by a police escort around the winding steep hilly streets of Monte Carlo. The centipedes of pedestrians were all flashing their cameras and cell phones as the kaleidoscopic procession of strange flat cars made their way downtown.

Finally, after all the cars had come in from going around a few times at the circuit de Monaco, all the competing teams pulled their vehicles into their respected display booths on the ground floor of the plush Fairmont Hotel. After Cody and his teammates wheeled their car on their platform they put it in park opening its doors and the hood.

"Where's Rick?" asked Cody, while taking off his helmet.

"He's at the monitor," said Eloi. "He hasn't been quite right for a while actually." He gently tapped Iarlaith on the shoulder. "Dennison even told us he was starting to have second thoughts for even coming here."

"Seriously?" The Dark Giant looked back to their engineer. "He seemed totally fine this morning. The competition's still beatable."

Cody then glanced around at the other manufacturer booths. They were far more sophisticated than theirs. All they had was themselves, the car and its platform, and a table and some chairs to sit in. The other booths, including Usangi-Kon's had all that as well as near food truck-sized plexus-glass displays, banners, female models flashing pearly white smiles, paraphernalia, and even projectors showcasing their car's features and performance.

"Well, we definitely look out of our league," said Cody while turning back to his men, "but we knew that since day one. Our win at last year's La Sarthe and partnership with Usangi-Kon should have been affirmation enough." He then looked back at Rick. "Maybe this is all starting to get to him, though."

"You should check on him, mate," said Iarlaith with a nod.

"Yeah, I'll do that."

He then took a couple of strides over to where Rick was standing. "You okay, Chief?" He stopped beside him giving him a friendly punch on his shoulder.

His old friend, however, remained silent staying glued to the T.V. above. Cody looked over to Lope who was accompanying him, and the expression he gave in reply was grim. Now the Dark Giant was concerned. Since their days in the Air Force together it was never common for Lope to show that something was rattling him, unless it was very serious. He looked back to Rick, who still had his eyes on the television. "What's this talk I hear from Dennison about 'second thoughts'?"

"I'll put it to you straight…" Rick paused, still looking up at the screen. "Actually if you look up at the roster now you'll see what I mean."

Cody then glanced up at the monitor and scanned the passing names on the bottom column of the screen. He kept observing until his stare froze in light of one of the drivers of Diederick Motorsports. "Wiebe Hramn?" he whispered to himself. He then looked over to his engineer. "Didn't you tell me he retired two years ago?"

Rick finally turned his eyes to his. "We both failed to check the final driving roster before we came here." He shook his head as he looked back up to the screen. "I figured two years of retirement would seal the desire of him ever returning to Nurburgring, or any racing for that matter. Let alone anyone else with the lack of marbles to take him on." He sighed while adjusting the silver rims of his spectacles. "I was wrong."

Cody looked away in thought while putting his hands on his hips. He just happened to glance at the Usangi-Kon booth and noticed Catherina was staring him. He was expecting maybe a quick wave, but the look she had in her eyes was unease. He even saw her glancing back and forth from the screen to him. *She must have seen the same thing* he thought. He then looked up at one of the many large white and rose gold chandeliers and took a deep breath. "Well, let's get it over with."

He returned his eyes to Rick. "Where's the Diederick booth?"

His old friend dropped his thick eyebrows in what appeared to be suspicion. The Dark Giant, for some reason couldn't understand what his concern was now.

"Why do you want to know?" asked Rick.

The answer of his friend's notion suddenly dawned on Cody. "I'm not looking to harm the guy if that's what you mean."

"But why do you want to know where his booth is?"

Cody was silent as he sincerely stared at his friend. Trust was something the Dark Giant took to heart, even in circumstances that made appeasing a vendetta to be the only clear motive.

"To forgive him," answered Cody. He then scanned around and finally found the platinum and black Diederick booth ahead. As he motioned to take a step, both Rick and Lope stood in his way pleading softly for him not to go.

"I'm good. I'm good," assured the Dark Giant, putting his hands up while scooting between them. His destination was a minute a way, minus the rather ordered sea of paparazzi and spectators he had to swim through. It was a little warm in the facility, which for most in the hotel was a charm since it was quite cool outside. In all truth,

Cody's heart was pure of any malice until he recognized a slender, pale man sipping a water bottle behind a table ahead. The temperature seemed to rise as he progressed, until he realized that the heat was actually from within.

The command, "Take care of my family, Chief!" played in his mind. Those were the last words his father screamed to Rick before his car plummeted to the asphalt. Anger was brewing, but the Dark Giant wouldn't have it. "You know my intentions, Jesus." he whispered to Him. "And I'm keeping them that way. I'm going to obey you." Though Cody meant what he said, the sincerity of wanting true reconciliation with Wiebe was slowly being zapped.

As he drew closer, he saw the slender man glance up and immediately look down. In fact, throughout this short encounter, the man would barely look up again. "Wiebe Hramn," said Cody as he stopped before the desk. He noticed Wiebe trembling as he held his bottle in what seemed like moral support. His father's murderer almost matched the picture he made of him that night back in Nicaragua, but he was a little smaller than he remembered. He was paler than he made him out to be, too, but his chiseled long face and piercing blue eyes didn't seem to fit his old epithet, die Schlange; German for "The Snake". He looked pitiful to him, like some scared puppy left in the rain. To his surprise, this moved Cody to pity him.

"My name is Cody Gregory Johnson, Junior, the son of Cody Gregory Johnson, Senior, the man you murdered sixteen years ago." Cody held out his hand. "Because my

Lord and Savior Jesus Christ freely gave me His forgiveness for my sins, so do I forgive you." His heart wasn't in any of those words, because this now became a cold ritual he had to get through. He didn't feel the Lord's power in his heart, or through his speech, and though he wouldn't have admitted it at the time, all he wanted from this was for Wiebe to show some sort of acknowledgment of what he did. But the man just sat in a chilled quiet. Cody still refused to pull back his hand, though the wait for any sort of response was a perpetuity.

Finally, he saw Wiebe raise his head slightly with his thin little mouth tremble in an effort to answer. "I am not responsible for your father's death," he said, lowering his head back to the ground.

This was enough to retract the Dark Giant's hand. He restrained his disappointment well with a very deep inhale followed by an even longer exhale. "Alright," said Cody. He slowly turned away. Before he could get a couple of steps forward he saw Catherina standing before him. Raising his eyebrow at the controlled anxiety in her stare, he noticed both his co-drivers were standing a few yards back watching. Just for curiosity's sake he took a look around the room just to see if anyone else was watching, and almost everyone, including most of the press had their eyes on him; even Michi. *Everybody must have put this event on the calendar, or something.* Cody looked back down to Catherina and held out his arms with a shrug. "Well, I tried."

As he put them down, Catherina gave a soft, yet nervous grin patting his side. With that they all walked away to the Judgment's booth.

CHAPTER SIXTEEN

The International Nurburgring Series consisted of six races; The 12 hours of Monaco, 12 Hours of Spa, 16 Hours of Suzuka, 24 Hours of Circuit de La Sarthe, 12 Hours of Bathurst, and the 12 hours of Nurburgring. The teams that earned the most points were the ones that emerged victorious at the season's end. A win guaranteed the most in a race, but unless a team won every single event in this highly competitive and costly sport, the amount of points they won consistently would win them the crown in the end. Thus all the competing teams would strategize which races they could afford to go all out while remaining conservative on races they couldn't.

For Team Judgment and Usangi-Kon, the best plan was to go all out at Spa and La Sarthe, while staying conservative, yet mildly competitive on locations that were outside of Europe, such as Suzuka and Bathurst. The scheme was mostly in favor for the Judgment team, for they hoped that their share of funds won from the victories would be enough to cover their travel costs outside of Europe. Traveling was not an issue for Usangi-Kon since they already had the resources to finance their commute without the need of any prize money. But both of their hopes paid off in the end. They won Spa and La Sarthe, taking both first and second in each race, while managing to finish in the top ten in the others. Both teams now had the points and the resources needed to be competitive enough to win the 12 Hours Nurburging, the I.N.'s grand finale.

It was early November in Nurburg, Germany, during one of the final mornings before race weekend, and teams Judgment and Usangi-Kon were preparing to do drills on the massive 12.9 mile Nurburgring Nordschleife Circuit. The day was cool and breezy, and the heaven's beams were excluded by the cold curtain of the mellow overcast sky. A day like this was much to Cody's liking. Fall was his favorite season, and any day, or time that was bereft of the sun satisfied him. He didn't like being hot and sticky, and since teething he always found the sun's glare a nuisance. While his car was getting its engine and tires warmed up the Dark Giant was sauntering along the tarmac that flanked the pit lane. He imagined a blur of metallic white passing down the track. The color of the last car his father drove.

He took a forkful of pumpkin pecan pie that Corina, Lope's wife, had baked for the team. As the crunchy, spicy, sweet filling caressed his tongue, he took a whiff of the crisp air. A soft breeze blew on his face as his eyes awoke to the vast and deep amber and orange sea of trees just over the fence and afar. He smiled as all that he chewed slid down his throat sinking heavy into his tummy.

All that's missing is the milk. He then felt a small, but firm impact on his ribs. As he looked down grasping his side with his free hand, there was little Catherina standing beside him gazing him with a smile. "I guess you'll have to do," he said with a grin.

As she raised her black and white rimmed shades from her eyes, she looked at the paper saucer in his hand and then back up to him. He knew that stare all too well; like a little girl looking up to her father for a bite. Cody rolled his eyes.

"You're so greedy, Cody," jeered Catherina slapping her hands on his stomach.

Not wanting to hear her complain about getting a small piece, he cut off a nice chunk with his fork. "I swear, you only want me for the food." Cody lowered the morsel into her mouth.

"Mmm," she moaned, while chewing in delight. "Yes, I only use you for my culinary fix. And I don't know how you can keep such strong abs. If I ate as rich as you, I'd roll as good as Perellis."

"Ha." Cody gave her a wink while taking another bite. "You gotta graze a little, Cat. Keeps the metabolism going."

"Yeah," said Catherina while stroking her hair, "including dead lifting 800 lbs. for reps.

Cody nodded in agreement while looking away. "Yeah, that too."

"Fat has no chance to hide with you, papi."

The two of them just stood side by side observing the forest. Catherina then held Cody's free arm while tugging it gently. "So what made you guys come up with the Judgment?"

Cody smirked with a chuckle. He glanced at Catherina, whose eyes met his at the same time. "You sure you want to know?"

Her silence suggested yes.

"Hm." He then returned his eyes to the scenery. "The idea was to build a car that was fast and devastating enough to beat Wiebe and embarrass the I.N. forever allowing him to continue racing in the league. Lope and I started sketching it a couple of weeks after we became bunk mates at Shepherd. We found out that we both liked cars and racing, and when I told him how my dad died, we both decided to make a car that would *avenge* his death. At first we wanted to make something really angry and vengeful. But the more we kept going at it, the more the Holy Spirit got involved. All the free time we had those years were spent on auto-cad making the car as aero-dynamic as possible. We talked composites, air-ducts, down force, fuel, displacement, diffusers. We were going to actually name it God's Car since our hearts had changed to making a car worthy of his His driving. We also felt the car's exterior had to have a sense of omniscience. Its presence had to be something that demanded reverence, like it should be the only car worthy to be on the track. And its performance had to be a complete translation of its appearance. That's how we finally came up with the name Judgment."

He paused as he beamed. "God's judgment on the auto-racing world."

"Well, you guys sure proved that last at year's La Sarthe," chimed Catherina. "350 mph average speed on the Mulsane. 6 lateral g in the Porsche chicanes. 2:38 lap time. One of the commentators even said, and I quote, 'Jesus is God if He can drive like that.' You know even Michi's eyes were bucking out of his head during your whole first stint?"

"Really," said Cody while returning his stare at Catherina. She gave a nod in affirmation. "Hm," he grunted while looking away. He took another forkful. "That must have been a hard pipe to smoke."

She snickered giving him another blow to the rib. "So when did the three of you have time to make the car?"

"We actually only made it two years ago"

"Really? When did you two leave the Air Force?"

"Well, after my sixth year there, I left for wrestling. Lope stayed. We only got in contact again a couple of years ago when we built it."

"But why so long? Did you guys have a falling out?"

Cody shook his head. "No. I just didn't keep up with him after I left. It was Rick who actually brought the three of us together."

"Rick knew Lope?"

"No. Rick first heard about Lope when I showed him the Judgment's designs. I was originally giving it to him to give away as a prize to one of our future pupils. But when he looked it over on his own, he was so convinced it could exist, he sought his racing constituents and colleagues for evaluation. The Lord then led him to Google up Lope. The rest's history."

Another calm fell on them as they stood together.

Catherina began to caress his arm. "Your father ever cross your mind?"

"Hm." Cody nodded as a smile emerged. A softness bloomed in his eyes. "Yeah, I did think of him." He glanced at Catherina, and their eyes met again.

"What was he like?"

"He was a true rascal," answered Cody while looking away. "That's what I remembered most about him. Always had this cocky grin on his face. Like any mischief he was about to get into he was going to pull through without a scratch. That's what mom said drew her to him most."

Another quiet came upon them as he then put the last piece of pie in his mouth.

"You think God would ever call you to share the Gospel with his murderer?" asked Catherina.

"I hope not," answered Cody, while emptying the crumbs from his plate onto the ground. "Forgiving him was hard enough. I don't think witnessing to him would fare any better." His eyes again met Catherina's. "But, hey, if that's what the Lord will have me do, I'll do it."

She smiled.

"What are you cheesing about?" he said as his expression slowly rhymed with hers. Looking into her eyes he believed he saw the answer. Something like a sun's warmth seemed to grow between them. He then wrapped his arm around her shoulder nestling her to his side. *She's like gold, this woman.*

CHAPTER SEVENTEEN

7:50 a.m. the following Sunday morning had finally arrived. It was race day and pretty much every competing team was trying to squeeze in as much last minute tweaks and strategy they could muster. For Cody, his team, and Catherina, however, this was their traditional time of prayer. After they had broken away, Catherina pounded his fist and headed back to her engineer. Cody then received kisses and hugs from both his mother and sister, followed with some words and pats on the back from Lope, Éloi, and Iarlaith. After he put his helmet on and slid into the Judgment, Rick was there to buckle him into his seat.

As his old friend was fastening his harness, Cody noticed his eyes seemed adrift. "What's up Chief?" asked Cody as he flipped on the switches.

"Déjàvu I guess." Rick rested his elbow on the door opening while gazing at the dashboard. "It's just like it was sixteen years ago, though I needed less room to strap down your father." Sorrow began clouding his old friend's eyes.

Cody managed to contort his right hand through the cramped space to plant it firmly on Rick's shoulder. "Don't forget where he is now, Chief."

His friend nodded. "I know," he choked. "It's all too easy for us believers to forget the grave's not our home. Just wish the Lord would have allowed us to enjoy him a little longer." Rick went back to fastening the straps. "Now stay beside Hramn until you see, or we tell you that Catherina's behind you. That'll prevent the Diedericks from drafting together in the beginning."

He then retracted his hands to the door seal. "If the Raffinatos give the number 44 Diederick enough friction, like I hope, it might make it easier for Catherina to get behind you sooner."

Cody gave a nod.

Rick then gave him a couple of taps on the helmet. "Go get 'em."

Several minutes later, after the pace car had finally led Cody and the rest of the competitors around the track, it pulled away to the left onto pit lane. Having pole again he was now leading all the other competitors down the extensively railed and timber-hedged Dottinger Hohe Straight.

"Gas, gas, gas," said Rick through Cody's ear phones.

The Dark Giant complied and with a heavier press of his size 18 foot the Judgment's metal heart growled from behind him pushing him forward.

At the end of the first lap, the leading seven cars came unto the long slightly banking Galgenkopf turn and Cody noticed in his side mirror one of the three Raffinatos veering into the road leading to pit lane.

"Catherina's moving up to fourth," said Cody's engineer.

"What's the complication with that Rafinato?" asked Cody.

"Overheard the commentators say it was having suspension issues."

"And then there were six." The Dark Giant and the following five competitors behind him were going all out down the suffocating track not willing to yield any ground. So synchronized and fluid was their movement in and through the corners that they seemed more like flat and loud futuristic ice skaters.

"I'm going to slow up to let the 44 Diederick get behind the 43," said Catherina through Cody's ear phones.

"You doing that could allow one of the Raffinatos to move in to take fourth," retorted Michi.

"It could be a gamble worth taking," said Catherina.

"She makes a good point, Squid," said Rick to Michi. "We need to start drafting now if we're to get any advantage on time when we pit."

"It's your call, chief," said Catherina.

They paused on the channel for a couple of seconds. "Okay, but do it just before you hit the Wehrseifien."

"Aye, aye Squid," said Catherina.

"Stay beside the 43, Cody," said Rick. "Don't pull away."

A minute later, they were all shooting out of the winding Kallenhard chicanes.

"Catherina slowed her car down," said Rick to Cody. "Let's see if the 44 Diederick took the bait."

Cody kept his eye on the invisible lines ahead to cut through the apexes of the long ever meandering turns. "He took the bait." said Rick. "The 44's moved in behind Wiebe."

While coming out of the Wehrseifien turn Cody looked over at the rear camera view on his dashboard and saw Catherina's green, black, and orange swirled striped Katsune moving in right behind him.

"Mush, Cody," said Catherina, "mush!"

Cody grinned as his teammate pulled into his slip stream. Their combined speeds began to push them further and further away from the Diedericks and Raffinatos.

Two laps later Cody and Catherina were more than four minutes ahead of the competition and were already beginning to lap the slower tiers. After they both left the pit for fuel, they were heading towards the Hochiechen turns, when one of the Tier Two Porches came out of the turn too aggressive, and drove off the track smashing its yellow rear bumber on the steel rail to the right.

"Wow," said Cody as he watched the car's carbon fiber wing shatter, and a fragment of it bombarded his windshield. The Dark Giant checked to see if his glass had any blemishes, and, to his dismay, he spotted a small crack in the upper right corner. "Chief, she's going to need a new windshield."

"Is there a crack?" asked Rick.

"Yeah, on the upper right."

Cody heard nothing from his engineer for a few seconds as he came towards the lake-size sand trap landmarking the sharp hairpin turn ending the Quiddlebacher straight.

"Yeah, Cody," answered his engineer. "You're going to have to bring it in. Lope said it'll shatter in just one more lap with these speeds."

"Why can't you just seal the glass?" asked Catherina.

"If we were driving on a much slower track we could get away that," answered Rick.

"Replacing the windshield instead of sealing it could cost us the race, and the championship," said Michi. "If he leaves her now she'll be dog food for the drafting of Diedericks and Raffinatos. Cody might even be a lap down before he comes back. It would take, and I say this sparingly, "a miracle" to get back in front of her in time."

"God does work miracles, Michi," said Rick.

Oh, boy, thought the Dark Giant with a soft snicker, *Michi's probably rolling his eyes right now.*

A few minutes later they all arrived on the Pflanzgarten II straight.

"Alright Cat," said Cody, "hold down the fort till I get back."

"Yeah, right," griped Catherina in Spanish, and Cody knew she had good reason to.

Her amazing Katsune GTR VF1, which had the flat round shape of a Mazda 787b and the pointy nose of a Peugeot 908, was a true tantrum in Veloce Formula. Yet, it's little, but potent 950 horse powered 6 rotary engine alone could not withstand for long the pursuit of two drafting Diediericks with 9 liter W16 engines making a combined horse power of 2400.

"Just keep your trust in Christ," encouraged Cody, "not in the situation."

A few minutes later Cody came into his garage stopping before the post man, and the crew team immediately rolled the car it inside. Two of his men then drilled the roof off and carefully replaced the now spider-webbed cracked windshield with a fresh new one.

As they were wheeling the Judgment out of the garage Lope, who was bringing the car out with other crew men, yelled to Cody through the window, "Let's let this cosmic beast preach its sermon!"

After the men had stepped away Cody geared the car off neutral with the tap of his paddles, and turned a blue knob on his steering wheel to pit control.

"Catherina is ahead of you by 5 minutes and 12 seconds," said Cody's engineer as he drove down pit lane. "God willing you should be behind the number 44 Diederick within three laps."

"God willing, indeed," whispered the Dark Giant. He felt in his heart that the race was already lost. A five minute gap was a huge hurtle for any driver to jump, even if they had 1450 horse power at their disposal. Unless, of course the driver wasn't human.

"Let me take the wheel?" said a voice.

"God?" whispered Cody. It was too clear to be from his ear piece, and it didn't belong to either Rick, Lope, Michi, or Catherina. *Why would He want to take the wheel? This is just auto-racing, after all?*

"Is this not my car?" answered God. "My *judgment* on the auto-racing world."

Cody was shocked that He actually chimed in on his thoughts. He never got used to the reality that God even knows and hears them, let alone if anyone gets used to it. He knew surrendering to Him didn't mean pulling over and getting out of the car, because He was already in him. It meant surrendering his will to His. Cody felt the Lord tug at his soul, but he knew that God wouldn't take full control, until he let Him. He took a deep breath, and through what can only really be described through feelings, gave control over to Him.

CHAPTER EIGHTEEN

Cody was still wide awake, or at least that's what he thought. He could see all around the cockpit, but he couldn't feel his body. He could see his hands moving the steering wheel, and he could see his feet tapping the clutch and the pedals, but he knew he wasn't moving them. It was now that he was certain that Jesus had dislodged his soul from his now tranced body, while He piloted the car.

Cody was not the only one to be transformed by this phenomenon. The Judgment's physique didn't change, but in a way it did. The saying form follows function had been completely reversed. The car now was not ominous because of its muscularly aggressive body, its apocalyptic voice, and its large headlights; it looked ominous because it was Ominous. Its headlights, now like bluish white lit eyes, seemed bent on others' obliteration. The two huge ducts besides its nose were now mistaken for two ravenous mouths. Its engine's screams now sounded like, well screams. It didn't appear to be a machine being driven with great dexterity, but instead a terrible beast abolishing the circuit.

The Cosmic Beast now soared so fast down the straights that its nose split the air making an aurora-like field to drape its body. Every time the car would lie up on the throttle without touching the brake it would let out a blue back fire from its 13 centimeter side exhaust that sounded more akin to a battle ship cannon round. With each turn it took its loss of speed was near none existent. It had no hesitation going in and out of the bends, as if a child's hand was racing its body on a toy track. Every competitor that was at least a mile of its coming could only hear its mighty bellow growing, and whenever they saw its approach, even the Tier Ones parted way to let it through.

The media was so amazed with its awesome presence and performance that all the screens just showed its footage. Some of the engineers and their administrators complained about not being able to see the coverage for their own vehicles, but most of them just watched in wonder of the Judgment's onslaught. They even tuned in to the car's audio as well, and it so drowned out every other engine on the track, that spectator's trackside or in front of the monitors forgot the other cars actually had one. But what startled everyone who could see the feed inside the cockpit and its gallop around the circuit was that it was anything but human. Many fellow racers and commentators alike respected Cody's skill with the car, but seeing him fluidly steering the wheel at such uncanny and hostile velocities on the most demanding and treacherous course in the world with no twitching left them spellbound. And with each lap the Judgment only went faster.

President Laurent, including everyone accompanying him in the room, even those who didn't care much for auto sports, stopped everything just to witness the Judgment on the screen. As time went on, the once bright gray sky got more and more troubled until it was almost pitch black. The clouds quickly became pregnant with water and fury, and the storm it birthed was worse. Lightening flashed, the gales tackled, and the meteors of water crashed down. All the competing cars on the track had unique L.E.D. designs on their headlights that made them look like flat space ships in the dark, but the Judgment's designs made it utterly ethereal. There were Hebrew characters wrapped around the back slopes of the car that glowed only at night that read, "Thy Kingdom Come, Thy will be done, On Earth as it is in Heaven." Its fire and lightening vinyl too began to luminate due to the aurora field covering it. The downpour didn't hinder the Judgment's performance, but in fact only seemed to make its presence even more menacing. Due to the immense wind it generated the rain was deflected within an half of an inch off the car's surface. The water also shaped around the car's winglets, and combined with the wide beam of its' circled eyes it took on the appearance of an immense electric white and orange dragon darting and snaking down the track.

Not a single soul that watched the screens paid any mind to anything else. It had their hearts, either through awe or fear. Even Michi couldn't look away. Rick, who was staring his monitor as well, was held fast by the Johnson women as they, and everyone else in the garage watched in amazement. As one of the commentators aptly surmised while leaping and dancing out of his seat in sight of Its glory, "God has visited us! The Lord has visited us! He's the One driving the machine!"

"Then the end has come, in Germany!" blurted out another in horror. No one heard the thunder, for the Judgment's dominant roar was all the sound one could hear. All the spectators outside who were huddled in their tents and vans couldn't even see their hands in front of them, but whenever the car flew by they had a streak of "day light" that lasted for a minute. The officials were so distracted by the footage, that the thought had never crossed their minds to stop the race due to the danger the other competitors might suffer from poor visibility and lack of grip, and because the down pour was so sudden no one had a chance to pit for wet-tread tires. But the Lord had accommodated for the other drivers through the Judgment's speed, for the heat it generated from its aurora kept the track dry, and the trail of light it left made it bright enough for everyone to see. Many believers in the garages, the official's booth, and outside fell to their knees, or danced while stretching out their arms shouting praises to Christ. There were even some nonbelievers that repented of their sins and trusted their lives to Him in light of His glory through the Judgment.

CHAPTER NINETEEN

Meanwhile the two Diedericks were several seconds away from closing in on Catherina. Wiebe Hramn, the driver of the number 43 car was ahead of Tiff, his teammate in the 44 as they both drafted together down the Brunchen turn.

"I'm losing grip in the rear, Crain." Wiebe heard his teammate say to his engineer. "It's getting loose around the esseses."

A moment of quiet passed on the channel. "Pit now for fresh tires," answered Tiff's engineer.

"You mean right now?" asked Tiff.

"Now. Our genius technician here felt it necessary to keep us uninformed of the possible puncture in the tire because *you only mentioned performance problems now.*"

"Ignore him, Tiff," said Wiebe. "Surely you can hold out for a lap more."

"I guess you can see his psi level on my screen, too!" yelled the engineer.

"From the looks of last year's season the Raffinatos showed you couldn't see much of anything," chided Wiebe. He then turned his voice back to Tiff. "If you leave now, the Judgment is sure to overtake me soon."

"I possibly have my life to consider, mate," said Tiff.

"Then be a coward and leave. Choose fear over victory."

"I didn't expect a man like you to value my life, being you're capable of taking one."

Wiebe spoke no more. As the two of them came unto the Galgenkopf turn Wiebe looked into his rear camera image and saw Tiff pull into pit lane. His demeanor had been stable throughout the race, yet for some reason the warmth seemed to leave him from the inside. The rear lights of Catherina's Katsune were just two seconds from his grasp. He was starting to hear a faint sound besides his own engine, but he paid it no mind. *Just a little more, maybe* he thought.

The faint noise now grew into an overwhelming howl, and it was growing louder and closer by the second. The frost within him began to spread throughout his body. *What on earth is that sound.* Wiebe knew that he and Tiff left the two Raffinatos long behind, and even if they had closed in on his now near minute lead on them, there was no way their small V6 diesel engines could possibly drown out his larger W16. He glanced down at the monitor on his dashboard and saw what looked like a ball of white light with two, even brighter, bluish white eyes. He blinked twice to affirm his doubt, but the form was still there and was approaching incredibly fast.

"The Judgment is behind you," said Wiebe's engineer, but his now shrunken heart only allowed him to hear "...Judgment is behind you."

The light before his windshield vanished as the onyx sky veiled his sight. Though the inside of his cockpit was still lit up by all the colored lights from his gages and switches, he saw nothing. Yet as the siren behind him grew louder white light began to flood his cabin. He looked at the rear camera view again and the once ball of white looked more like a being inflamed in an orange, blue, and white brilliance. His roll cage, as well as every instrument in the cabin started to rattle, and when he glanced at what little he could see of his hands they were rocking the wheel like a record on a turn table. He knew such erratic steering at his speed would have sent anyone airborne, but even though he still couldn't see the road ahead he felt grounded, somehow. As the creature left the rear view, Wiebe glanced over to his right side mirror and saw it starting to flank him. Its eyes even appeared to look at him as it came closer. He looked away closing his, as even the rubber-like percussions from his heart were engulfed by Creature's voice. He willed to put his foot over to the brake pedal, but it somehow froze to the accelerator. He opened his eyes again and all he could see was a blinding white about him. Turning to his right again the Judgment's body was now completely beside him. As he peered through its electric rainbowed-water flowing swathe, he saw strange characters glowing blue on its back. His mind was immediately taken back to a time in Sunday school when he remembered his teacher reading aloud of when King Belshazzar saw writing on the wall.

My time has come. Wiebe fainted as the iota of courage he had drained out of his bowls.

"**WHAT DO YOU FEAR, WIEBE HRAMN?**" said a clear, firm voice in German.

Wiebe blinked. Opening his eyes he could now see the road ahead and all light had returned to his cockpit. His body was completely numb from shaking, but his cabin was sound again. He looked up ahead for the creature, but all he saw was the Judgment ahead of him and pulling away.

CHAPTER TWENTY

Cody was lodged back into his body like a glove, and though he could see everything happening while God took control, he felt as if he had just woken up when he regained function of his brain.

"Cody!" yelled Catherina.

"Huh?" Cody blinked as he tightened his grip on the wheel. The volume of his sense of surroundings were steadily being dialed up. He felt the urge to explain to his teammate the condition he was in, but he knew telling of a Holy Spirit induced trance would be too much for everyone over the channel to grasp. "Did you miss me, Cat?"

"Miss, you? I've been calling your name ever since you were behind me. How on Earth did get to me so fast? That down pour was horrible. I had no visibility, and then the next second, there was enough light through the dark to see the road ahead. I had plenty of grip, too; like it didn't even rain. So strange."

The Dark Giant's eyes lit up in fear. *Really?* He knew expressing this aloud would raise all kinds of questions. How could he be surprised of this news, let alone this being news at all to him, since in their eyes he was on the same track at the time. "Praise, God," was the only words he could think to say as they drafted together down the straight.

A lap later the Judgment, the Katsune, the Raffinatos, and the 43 Diederick all pulled into pit lane for their mandatory stop. As Wiebe stopped his car before the post man he began to unfasten his harness.

"What are you doing?" asked his engineer as Wiebe hoisted himself out of his seat. "You've still got forty minutes left to your stint!"

Mr. Hramn paid him no mind as he started to walk off. As his engineer waved for the other driver to take his place, Wiebe took off his helmet and ski mask dropping them both to the ground, and left out of the garage.

CHAPTER TWENTY ONE

Teams Judgment and Usangi-Kon went on to win the 12 Hours of Nurburgring coming in at first and second. With this, they claimed both the International Nurburgring Drivers and Constructors Championships. On the following Monday evening after their victory the I.N. President and all his trustees took the entire racing staff of both Judgment and Usangi-Kon to dinner at the Restauration Kopernikus, in Nuremburg, Germany.

During the festivities, Cody's waitress stopped by asking him if he wanted anything else.

"Another Pfannenschnitzel," answered Cody. His waitress' eyes jumped.

"That's your third one, Cody," said Catherina, who was sitting snug to his right.

"Hey, everyone should be allowed to have one day out of many to indulge." He took a sip of pumpkin ale from his giant mug. "What better time than today."

"Dumping all that cream, starch, and pork in your veins isn't good for you, papi."

"I know. That's why I did that two hour circuit workout with you before coming here. All this pork here's gonna repair these torn muscles."

Catherina paused from her hopeless pursuit in reasoning with him while taking a sip of Champagne. "And what about all those potatoes, and breadcrumbs? Last time anyone checked, starch wasn't protein."

"I gotta replenish all those calories I burned somehow."

"Looks like you don't need me as your conscience with this seniorita around, Cody," said Nadie.

"Might as well stop while you got breath, honey," said Algoma. "Gluttony is not a sin my brother plans on repenting from anytime soon."

"You calling me a glutton, Possum," said Cody. He then pointed his thumb back to Catherina. "You should have seen this girl back in Nicaragua. What was that, about 15 tonic pineapples you drank?"

"Six," said Catherina, slapping his hand away.

The waitress had just arrived with his plate.

"Man, you guys must have this on tap." He softly shoved Catherina with his shoulder teasing her with his tongue. She rolled her eyes as he took his clean silverware out of the new napkin. He was just about to start his third trip down that velvety, mushroom-sauced pork escapade when President Theirii, who sat to his left, stood up from his seat tapping his glass with his fork.

After everyone had quieted down Laurent spoke, "I would like to take the time to brag about who I feel is the greatest racer…"

He stopped while looking down and around at everyone in the room. As an anxious grin dawned on his face he choked, "Excuse me; one of the greatest racers I've ever met, Cody Gregory Johnson, Junior." Cody nodded in appreciation as he heard the applause spread around the room. "I don't say that he's one of the best because of how fast and well he drives the Judgment; though he shattered almost all the tracks' all-time records this year in all categories."

As some of the audience chuckled, the president continued, "No, no. Honestly, he's one of the greatest because to me he's a superb example of it being a good thing that the apple doesn't fall too far from the tree. Like his father, he's a racer of good character who wins free of any shenanigans."

The president then paused for a second as his cheerful demeanor fell to something more solemn. "He didn't even stoop low enough to take what was rightfully his."

As Cody looked up at him the vice president tried to reason with his boss to go no further, but Laurent waved him off. "It's time to be frank, or its time to be real as you Americans would say. And since we're talking about an American I guess the latter expression fits best."

Mr. Theirii turned his head to Cody's, and while shaking his head in disbelief, continued, "We don't know how you did that miracle with that car yesterday, but the moment you pulled up beside Wiebe I would have done that snake what he did to your father. And I would have gladly looked the other way..."

Laurent shook his head again wiping a tear from his cheek. "But like your father you're a better man than most. Being the good Christian man you are, you're going to give that kudos to God aren't you?"

As the Dark Giant nodded yes, Laurent placed his hand down on his shoulder. "Auto-sports could use more men of you and your father's caliber. For what it's worth, God bless the ministry that you and Mr. Gora are building."

A couple of claps peeked out until it poured into an all-out applause.

The president held out his hand to the Dark Giant, and Cody stood up and shook it. "Thank you Mr. Theirii," whispered Cody.

"No, thank you," said Laurent.

"Give us a speech, Kodiak," he heard Eloi shout. His teammate banged his fist on the table, chanting, "Speech! Speech! Speech!"

Cody shook his head while waving his hand no, but everyone throughout the tables started to carry on the chant. He then noticed Catherine snag his plate to herself grinning at him daringly. Cody gave her a pout. He knew that she knew that all he wanted was to sit down and eat the delicious food on his plate.

Not being able to resist the crowd's wooing any longer he held up his hands in surrender. "Okay, okay." He then whispered to Jesus under his breath, "Lord, what would you have me tell them?"

After the assembly quieted down Cody, through the Holy Spirit, said, "I shouldn't be here today." While some of the men at the tables joked around saying whatever, Cody continued, "It's just true, I shouldn't be here. I didn't think I'd ever be here, come think of it. A couple of years ago I was content with just going around Cotulla and other counties in Texas evangelizing the Gospel of Jesus Christ with my church and the Texas Open Air Campaign. I was cool with never being in the victory circle, let alone on the grid again."

Cody nodded to Catherina. "I'm still recovering from taking guilt trips, so if you see Cat ribbing me, it's out of love."

As Catherina grinned, while some in the crowd laughed, the Dark Giant continued, "Couple of years back, Rick told me about a vision God gave him of producing racers that reflected God's character on and off the track. See God stated His plan for man in Genesis 1:26, 'Let us make man in our image, in our likeness.' In translation that means our sole duty in this world is to reflect who He is. Not lying, not committing adultery…"

Cody then looked at Laurent holding his hand out, "…not murdering…." the president nodded in agreement. Cody looked back to the crowd, "…not stealing, honoring your parents are all reflections of God's character. Jesus expects us in all things, and in all activities to reflect Him, so

Rick and I thought, why not teach people to reflect His character in racing as well?

"But when Chief asked *me* if I would race the car that Lope and I designed I was hesitant. You see a few years back I took all things pertaining to racing out of my life so I could maintain God as my life's focus. I feared if I said yes I'd be committing idolatry all over again. After taking this offer before the Lord in prayer for a couple of weeks, I had a talk with my pastor at our church's annual summer picnic. While throwing a football back and forth with some teens, the subject of sports for some reason," Cody raised his arm and tightened his bicep, "came up." Some in the audience, particularly the women laughed and oohed. Cody smirked, lowering his arm with a shrug. "Baseball was his sport. He was aspiring to go pro, got a scholarship for Stanford. He was even elected to play for the Cape Cod League. If any college baseball player wanted to be noticed by MLB scouts, that was the chance to have. But he tore his right A.C.L., shattering a good opportunity. He was frustrated with God about allowing this to happen, but he recalled asking God before it did if He would take the sport out of his life if it would get in the way between them. He sought the Lord strong during his recovery, and through the years God revealed to him that the clergy was to be his vocation.

"So when I asked him if he caved into his desire for baseball by joining the La Salle County Softball Church League, he said something that stuck with me; Some desires of the heart we have will never be fulfilled, nor will we be allowed to return to them because God knows it will hinder

Him from being our delight. But, sometimes if He sees that you have matured in obedience to Him and only desire to worship Him with what He gives you rather than worship the things He provides, in His grace He'll give you a second chance because He knows that you will worship Him with the desire given you, instead of worshipping the desire itself. Psalm 37:4 says that if you delight yourself in the Lord He will give you the desires of your heart. Well, I stand before you all today as an example of someone He's given a second chance to worship Him with their desire."

Cody raised his hand in finish, and everyone around the room applauded him. After shaking hands with the president he looked at Catherina in playful intimidation while pulling back his plate from her with his finger. His love, however just smirked resting her chin on her hand as he sat back down.

CHAPTER TWENTY TWO

After everyone had had their fill of merriment that night, the I.N. administrative staff dropped Teams Judgment and Usangi-Kon off at the Hotel Zur Burg. From there Lope and his wife took Nadie and Algoma back to their home in Munster. The remaining racing and administrative staff from both teams went off to their respected rooms for the night, as well. While Cody was upstairs chatting with Catherina by her door, he spotted her engineer out of the corner of his eye standing on the stairs.

"How long you been spying on us, Michi?" asked Catherina as she playfully looked back.

"Long enough, chipmunk," answered Michi.

Catherina then flipped her head back to Cody's. "Well wine, pork, and starch have always been a great recipe of fatigue for this girl." She then raised her chin for a kiss, and Cody eagerly leaned down to answer her request. "God willing we'll see each other up tomorrow?"

"God willing," said Cody with a beam.

Catherina grinned as she opened her door. "Good night, Kodiak. Night, Squid." She waved bye while stepping into her room.

As his love closed the door, Cody turned around giving a short bow to Michi. "Good night, Mr. Makoto." He turned around and started to walk away.

"Mr. Johnson."

"Yeah?" said Cody about-facing in a soldier's heel spin.

Michi, started to approach him with his hands in his pockets. "Big man, there's something I wanted to tell you."

"Now that's an anomaly."

"Hm," grunted Michi with a smirk.

The much smaller and older man stopped before him looking up at him with his small brown sloth-like eyes. He had a hard charm in that tanned wrinkled broad face that was buried under his long thick scraggly gray and white beard. Cody never got much of a chance to notice that before.

"Yeah, I'll admit I've seldom said a word to you. Being the Darwinian atheist I am, from the day I met you I dismissed you simply for your race and religion. I did the same to Catherina at first, which I'm sure she probably told you."

Moved by the Holy Spirit Cody asked, "What made you become an atheist, if you don't mind me asking?"

Michi's face was troubled immediately. "Who are you to question one's upbringing? Did I do that to you?"

Cody too returned a perplexed stare. "One's upbringing and personal belief are two different things. Just because Goma and I were brought up in a Christian household doesn't make us Christian. I'm sure you'd agree we had to cross that bridge on our own when we got there."

"Hm." Michi still stared at him, but Cody could see that he was recessed in thought. He then stroked his beard as if it was his muse. "My parents were butchered by Yakuza when my brother and I were little. We were small enough to hide from them until they left. We had to fend for ourselves ever since. I didn't believe in a god back then, and ridiculous myths they taught in school about man being the crud scraped out of some goddess' eye fitted reality perfectly. So when my hierarchs had me stay through your interview at last year's La Sarthe it was, to be frank, an aneurism for me. But one thing you said stuck with me; That none of us want God in our lives anyway, and that had your father's murderer worshipped God instead of his own ambitions at the time your father might still be here."

Cody was amazed that Michi took that away from what he said that afternoon a year ago. He remembered being reluctant to even being at the press conference believing it was just typical self-promotion. But the little shred of Gospel he got to share struck this man the most.

Michi paused as his eyes drifted to the floor. "Maybe if those men knew God they wouldn't have murdered my parents. Maybe if my neighbors knew God they would have taken a couple of wet-nosed orphans in instead leaving us to eat from trash cans and scrub toilets to exist."

Michi then glanced back up at Cody. "So what lead you be a Christian? Let me guess," he smirked with cunning pointing his finger to him, "you were afraid of going to H, E, double hockey sticks, yes?"

Cody nodded with a grin. "Yeah."

"Ha." The scruffy old man nodded his head. "That's the same thing Cat said. He sure does use fear to make His believers obey. I thought He was a God of love."

"He is, but He leaves it to you to accept His love, and that's what I did."

"Hm." Michi folded his arms, while nodding his head. "Maybe I'm coming to believe now that something or *someone unseen* does exist in You, Rick, and Cat, causing you all to speak and behave the way you all do. I believe now that at least you all are genuine followers of your God."

"Well, thank you. I appreciate that." He gestured his humility with his hands. "We're just following our Maker's design. All the credit goes to Him."

"Why's that?"

"Well, you said it yourself that someone unseen is causing us to behave the way we do. When a person makes Jesus their God, He comes and lives inside of us and empowers us to resist our innate evil urges. He gives us the will to obey and grow in obedience to Him."

"Hm." Michi stroked his beard again. "Catherina said something similar like that to me, but I don't understand why "God" Himself would come, or have to come and live inside you."

Cody saw that the small engineer was a little eager in the eyes to leave. But, making a gamble he asked, "Would you like me to explain?"

"No," said Michi, waving his hand, "I'm too tired to go deep into pontification."

"Okay."

The two of them stood with each other silently for a moment, until Michi looked up to him and held out his hand. Cody lowered his brows in confusion *Is this real?* He thought.

"I can assure you, Cody," said Michi, "it's quite real." Cody then grabbed hold of Michi's tiny but calloused hand, and they shook. The scruffy engineer then tipped off his large red squid emblemed skull cap to the Dark Giant. "Good night, Johnson."

"Good night, Makoto." Michi then turned away and walked down the hall.

CHAPTER TWENTY FOUR

The next morning, Cody was sitting on his bed finishing up the last chapter of his morning Scripture reading. He then put his Bible and MP3 player on his dresser and while leaning on it he prayed to the Lord for His guidance throughout the day. Suddenly a firmness emanated through his stomach. He knew it wasn't from the feast from last night, though it should have been. Taking one of his hands off the dresser he pressed his abdomen seeing if the pressure would either intensify or diminish. It did neither. *This is spiritual.* His face became troubled wondering what this could be. Usually any time this feeling would come about he knew it was Jesus warning him of something grave ahead, or Him pointing for him to share the Gospel with someone. "What is it, God?" He then looked up to the door, and feeling the Spirit directing him to go out he did as that.

Already dressed in a white T-shirt and a pair of beige khakis he came out of his room and stood in the hallway looking to and fro. *A little too quiet out here.* As he headed down to the white and gray staircase and made his way to the front lobby he saw that it, as well as the reservation desk, were both empty. *This a dream?* He then wandered towards the cafeteria and saw to his left that everyone in the hotel, including all the staff were crowded like ants into the lounge looking at the news on the large flat T.V. above. Seeing Rick,

Catherina, Michi and everyone from both their teams looking on along with everyone else, he walked over to them excusing himself through the crowd.

"What's going on, Chief?" asked Cody

"Just look at the screen," answered Rick.

Cody looked up and saw what looked like a drenched Wiebe sitting in the floor window of a tower in a large stone castle. The language was in German, but the captions were in English and French, and he read that the person they were covering was definitely Wiebe Hramn.

"We knocked on the door for you to come," said Iarlaith, "but you were too sound asleep."

"How long's this been going on?" asked Cody

"About an hour," answered Catherina.

The Dark Giant looked at the captions again and saw that Wiebe had dowsed himself with gasoline declaring that he was going to light himself on fire at 1:40 p.m. He glanced at the clock on the lower right hand corner on the news and saw that it was 12:20 p.m. Cody turned back to Rick. "Why's this guy going through with this?"

'"To leave this pathetic world in his prime with blazing glory." At least that's what he told one of the caretakers of the castle to say to the press."

Cody's phone rang, and when he dug it out of his pocket he saw that it was Lope. He then flipped it open while holding his hand over his other ear. "Yeah, Grey Hound."

"You see what's happening, Cody?" asked Lope.

"Yeah, I do."

"What's up with this guy?"

"I don't know, but we should all start praying for him now."

"Yeah, we have. We've all been praying in and out since we saw this. I just took some time out to see if you knew what was up, which now I see you do."

"And, Goma?"

"She's been on the coach watching the event the whole time. We invited her for prayer, but she refused."

"I understand. Well, I'll let you go, and I'll start praying with some of the folks here."

"Alright, you do that."

They both said 'bye' and Cody hung up the phone. He then went over to Rick and Catherina, putting his hands on both their shoulders. "You guys want to start praying for Jesus to deliver this man?"

Rick and Catherina agreed, and the three of them stepped out of the room into the lobby and started praying.

CHAPTER TWENTY THREE

Thirty five minutes later Cody, Rick and Catherina were still in prayer outside the cafeteria. "Help!" shouted a high pitched voice from around the corner. "Staff, help!"

What's up with this dude, thought Cody while the person kept pressing the bell at the reservation desk? As Cody opened his eyes to see what was happening he saw a staff heading towards the desk. He then returned his attention back to God and closed his eyes in prayer again. Another moment of quiet followed.

"Cody Gregory Johnson, Jr." Cody felt someone firmly tugging his arm.

He opened his now perturbed eyes. He absolutely hated being disturbed in prayer. "Excuse me, Jesus." When he turned around to see who it was, he saw a pale slender red-headed man. Cody failed to restrain his angst. "Do I know you?"

"Sorry," said the intruder, "I'm so sorry to disturb you Mr. Johnson, but I need to speak to you in private, now."

"Can this wait? We're in the middle of prayer."

The man firmly grabbed hold of Cody's arm. "It's most urgent, sir."

The man's desperation seemed to outweigh Cody's pursuit for prayer. In fact it felt as if the Spirit was urging him to go with him. "Okay," consented the Dark Giant and he followed him into the lobby.

"I'm Adalwolf Hramn," said the slender man as the two of them stopped before the reservation desk, "Wiebe's younger brother."

"What?"

Adalwolf then pulled out his phone from his jacket pocket. "He sent me this text at 8:23 a.m. this morning. Read it."

Cody took hold of it and looking into the small screen it read:

> I hoped the one I've wronged would have had the courage to do to me what I could not do for myself. Making a promise to a crowd for my dismissal from this cold world should be the key. Some say peer pressure is a great surrogate for moxy.

"I believe he's talking about you." said Adalwolf.

"Why?" Cody held out his hands in surprise. "How'd you come to that?"

"Well, almost everyone thought that you were going to kill my brother the way he killed your father. He's never been the same since then, and he only got worse after retirement. I figured from reading the text that he was hoping you were the one who would put an end to all of it."

Cody looked behind and saw both Catherina and Rick approaching them. "Why did you feel the need to show me this now?"

"For some reason, I believe you're the one that could talk him out of suicide."

"So you believe that the guy who your brother "expected" to kill him is now the best man to save him?"

"Look, I know it doesn't make much sense, but I figured that the last person he would hope to see would be the one person he would want to talk to."

Cody stroked his chin in thought.

"I know what he did to you and your family was absolutely horrible. But for the sake of my brother's life, please leave your grudge with him in the past."

Cody calmly locked eyes with him. "If I did have a grudge against him, would it be your place for you to tell me when to let it go?"

Adalwolf stood still, and spoke no more.

"I need to think this over."

He then turned around and walked over to Catherina and Rick. When the two of them asked the Dark Giant who the man was Cody explained everything to them.

"Good night," said Rick with his glasses jumping of his face. "Are you serious? Why you?"

While pointing his thumb back to Adalwolf, Cody answered, "He believes that Wiebe seeing the last person he expected to see could be the one guy to talk him out of it."

Catherina stared at him intensely. It was same stare she gave him that night in Nicaragua. Yet fear had not found Cody this time with that look, for it always came when she was concerned about him.

"What's wrong?" he asked.

"You're actually thinking of going up there to him aren't you?" she asked.

Cody gave a so-so nod. "Sort off."

She looked away sighing while shaking her head. Returning her eyes to him she said, "Cody, that man's extremely unstable and hostile. He's got gasoline all over him. You know he's armed? He used his gun to coerce the caretakers to get him up the there."

"I know. I know it's dangerous, but we know where we're going when we die; Wiebe may not know."

"Then I'm going with you," she said while folding her arms.

"You can count me in, too," chimed Rick.

"Alright. I want to pray with you guys first, though. The sign from God for me to go to him will be if he signals with his hand for me to come up. If he doesn't I'll know it's not from Him for me to go up."

"Alright," said Catherina.

Rick then nodded his head in agreement, and they all bowed their heads in prayer.

A few minutes later after they had finished praying they all came to Adalwolf. "Let's go," said Cody.

Adalwolf gave a quick nod and led them out to his car.

CHAPTER TWENTY FOUR

Thirty minutes later, Adalwolf pulled up to the crowded castle gate, and the four of them stepped out of the car making their way through the crowd. As they headed to the officers accompanying the Hramn family, Cody noticed amongst the people that some of them were actually holding signs in favor of Wiebe's driving prowess, and were even chanting in encouragement for him to go through with his plans. When some of them saw the Dark Giant's coming they booed him.

"Ask my brother if he would allow Cody to come up to talk with him," said Adalwolf to the officer before him.

When the officer turned around to Cody he almost fell back in alarm. "Why he has to be the biggest and darkest..." softly babbled the officer. The Dark Giant heard every word, but he was used to such reactions from Caucasians. He took no offense in his heart toward the officer, but he could see the shame in policeman's eyes from his utterings. "Excuse me," said the officer while waving his hand for mercy, "forgive me, sir of my rash words." He returned his now anxious eyes to Adalwolf. "Why do you want to send him?"

As Adalwolf explained himself to the policeman, Cody noticed a tall middle aged woman approaching him. "I recognize you." she said. "You're the son of the man my

Wiebe killed. Why would you want to talk him out of killing himself?"

"Because your son wanted me to." answered Cody.

She then looked to her son. "Did you really ask him to go up there?"

"Yes, I did." answered Adalwolf.

"Why?"

"There's no time for explanations now, just action."

"Well I demand an explanation, before an action," said the officer. "I'm not going to send a man up there that lost a loved one to him. Old animosities will arouse with tragic repercussions. It's a catastrophe waiting to happen."

"He could have made it tragic during their last race, Adler," said the other policeman standing beside them. "I follow the I.N. This man went as far to forgive Wiebe publicly before the season even started in February. If he wanted Wiebe to die he could have watched this at home or stood amongst the spectators waiting for '1:40' to come around."

"There's no threat in asking him," reasoned Adalwolf to Officer Adler.

Adler returned his eyes back to Cody. "You know he's drenched himself in petrol. He's got a gun too, you know; possibly loaded."

"I know," said Cody.

"And why would you be willing to risk your life to save the hide of your father's murderer?"

"Because his brother asked me to," replied Cody.

The two officers and even the Hramns stared bizarrely at him when he said this, but Cody continued, "God's given me success in talking people out of taking their own lives. And I know that if I do die in the process of trying to negotiate with him, at least I'm going to Heaven."

Adler stared at Cody for a moment, as if to question if him and his words were real. When he seemed convinced it was, the officer then rose up his intercom looking up Wiebe.

"Mr. Hramn!" said Adler.

As Wiebe looked down to him, the officer asked, "Your brother has sent Cody Johnson, Jr. to talk with you. Will you allow him to come up?"

Wiebe was still for a moment, until he nodded 'yes' and waved his hand in approval.

Adler looked back at Cody. "It's your show now. May your God be with you."

"I'm with God." said Cody. "But, thank you."

As he tried to step forward, Catherina firmly grabbed hold of Cody's hand. The Dark Giant looked down to her, and saw her eyes moisten. And to his astonishment, a smile slowly emerged. "Looks like that task's been given to you after all."

Cody was puzzled from what she meant, yet when it finally clicked in his brain, his face rhymed with hers. "Yeah, I guess it has."

Catherina then embraced him as strong as she could and Cody wrapped his arms around her raven head. As she released him he leaned down and pecked a kiss on her forehead.

Rick then came forward and hugged Cody, and whispered in his ear, "May God grant both of you a safe return."

"God willing," said Cody as he pulled himself away from both his friends. His eyes, too, moistened being moved by their concern, but he allowed not a tear to roll down his face as he approached the castle.

CHAPTER TWENTY FIVE

Minutes later, Cody trudged upward groping his hand along the cold moist stones that spiraled up the steps of the unlit tower. A steady draft carried the reek of petroleum down to his nose. As it intensified he knew he was nearing the top. All the while he prayed to the Lord for Wiebe's deliverance and His words to minister to him.

When he finally emerged through the doorway of the top floor, the light flooded his sight. *Why did they choose such high places to take their lives* he pondered, while squinting away the fumes' burn. As his eyes absorbed the light, he saw a dark lone hunched figure come to form.

There he was, Wiebe Hramn, his father's murderer sitting nearly dormant in the window. *The one thing I wanted to happen to this guy is the very thing I'm trying to stop him from doing.* The Spirit burned in him. "Sorry, God," he said rubbing his chest. "Just wanted to relish the irony a bit." The weight was heavy on the lone man; so heavy that Cody felt it. He also felt demons rustling about the room as well as the cringing air they carried. Feeling this again reminded him of what a fellow evangelist back in Texas told a kid who loved horror movies; just as trash attracts rats, so does evil entertainment attract demons. These wicked beings loved any activity that celebrated hopelessness or tragedy, especially, as Cody came to realize recently, suicide. This time, however the Lord moved for him to rebuke them, and not wanting to frighten Wiebe into a plummet He whispered in Jesus' name for them to leave. They did.

Cody then came behind the troubled man still flapping his eye lids from the fumes. He was at least grateful he didn't now have to endure both the evil spirits' nauseating presence and the burning aroma. Cody then stopped behind Wiebe while burying his hands in his pants' pockets.

"What's on your mind, Mr. Hramn." asked the Dark Giant.

He saw Wiebe's head bobble. He didn't even turn to see him. "What a strange inquiry for such an occasion." answered Wiebe. "What brings you up here, Johnson?"

"Adalwolf brought me here."

"Hm." Wiebe, for a moment, delayed his reply. "My parents did not name him "noble wolf" for nothing. That's what his name means in our language." Wiebe paused again, raising his dripping head to the overcast sky. "I need to do this world and my family a favor." With his free hand he caressed his long neck. "I was hoping you would have done me that favor two days ago." He fell silent again.

Cody took long breaths to relieve his impatience. He was completely confident that the Lord desired to deliver this man, but from experience he knew it did not always come in haste.

"How could you forgive the murderer of your own father?"

The question snapped him back into focus. "If I recall, you said you weren't responsible for my father's death?" answered Cody.

"Ha. Touché." Wiebe gave a heavy sigh which lead to another pause. "Those thoughts that brash 19 year old had back then. "Victory can't slip from me now. Not today! He's right there! Just one tap won't hurt. Cody's a veteran driver. He'll save his car. He won't die..." Wiebe wagged his head. "As soon as I crossed the finish line I heard Bang." He clapped his hands together insinuating the sound.

The incident flashed instantaneously in Cody's mind, and his calm composure buckled. *Keep me focused on you, Christ,* he prayed.

"I remember looking at the fire in the mirror; my heart froze. Kept hoping it was someone else. I pulled over to the grass along the Dottinger *knowing* Johnson was going to pass by..." Wiebe sniffled while raising his head. "Nothing."

Wiebe was silent again for a moment resting his free hand on his scalp. "Racing and winning were the only things that kept my mind off from what I did that Sunday, but when I retired my mind kept haunting me. I failed many times to end it. Just didn't have the guts to follow through."

Wiebe recessed again dropping his head. "When January came around and I saw that you were racing in this year's I.N. I thought my salvation had finally come. I figured I'd use your hatred towards me to put an end to this guilt. My just punishment..." Wiebe then turned his head over to

Cody's direction. "Why did you listen to my brother? You really wish me to stay alive?"

Cody straightened himself up taking a deep breath, and since the wind was blowing into the tower, the fumes didn't go down his throat. "You staying alive isn't my concern. Where you'll end up if you kill yourself is what concerns me."

Wiebe snickered, while looking away. "I know you did not come up here to share that HEAVEN and HELL stuff did you? Tell it to the wind."

"The wind doesn't have ears and it doesn't have to worry about its eternal destination, but you do. You know where you're going when you die?"

"Yep," sneered Wiebe, "worms and dirt."

"That's where your body goes. What about your soul? Where's that going to go when your body's buried?"

"Hell," said Wiebe nonchalantly. "You came all the way up here just to tell a man with a loaded gun and a body covered in petrol about God's wrath?"

"Is that where you want to go?"

Wiebe then looked over to Cody again. His eyes were startled. "You mean I really have a choice?" He then wagged his head. "I know what you're going to say next. You're going to tell me that I need to ask Jesus to forgive me of my sins *so I could go to Heaven*, right?"

"Is that what you want?"

Wiebe paused as his face went blank. He shook his head, again. "I take no weight to that rubbish. I left that behind at Sunday School."

"Well if you believe that the grave is all that awaits you, why not go through with it? What's to fear in sleep?"

Wiebe said nothing while dropping his head again. He then spoke, "I need to pay for what I did."

"I agree. You should pay for what you did, and God agrees with you on that, too. The wages of sin is death, both physical and spiritual. But out of His grace He's willing to give you the means to avoid it."

"I want Hell."

"Why?"

"Because I deserve it."

Full of the Holy Spirit, Cody then held out his hands in mocking agreement, "Well, if you feel you'll get relief from your guilt there, then go on and start the fireworks. Why wait till 1:40? I won't stop you."

Wiebe gave no reply with his head still left to a dangle. Another stillness befell them. Calling his bluff the Dark Giant came beside him, and leaned on the stone opening with his forearms. "Give me the gun and lighter."

Wiebe gave a silent resistance, but he gave in slowly handing them both to Cody.

The Dark Giant dropped the lighter on the ground stomping it with the heel of his gray Heritage boot, shattering it into wet shards. He also took all of the bullets out of the revolver and emptied them on the floor.

As Cody slung the gun across the room Wiebe asked him, "Why would God want to forgive a murderer?"

"Because He's merciful."

"I don't want his mercy."

"Why?"

Wiebe was silent for a moment as his usual dead pan face fell to a frown. "It's not fair."

"You're right. Mercy definitely means withholding what you deserve."

"I don't believe God forgives murderers."

"Why's that?"

"What do you mean by 'why's that'? Everyone hates murderers. Why would God forgive a murderer, especially one who murdered someone who believed in Him?"

"You ever read the Bible before?"

"No."

"You should. You see God had forty men under His influence write all books of the Bible, and they were split up into two Testaments; Old and New. One of those authors' names was Paul. Now Paul wrote more than half of the New Testament, but before he became a believer of Jesus and did all this, he was called Saul, a man who hunted down God's own followers and had them thrown in prison. He witnessed the stoning of a man of God named Stephen and did nothing to stop it, but approved of it. In fact, even hating someone is murder before God. That alone makes one worthy of Hell."

Wiebe raised his eyebrows in surprise. "That's pretty much everyone on earth."

"That's right." Cody nodded while giving a soft tap on Wiebe's his shoulder. "See God doesn't judge people according to other people, but according to Himself. He said that no one is good except God alone."

"Well if that's the truth about how He feels, then everyone's going to Hell."

"That indeed is where everyone deserves to go, but that's not the way it has to be."

"So a man can do whatever he wants and not have to pay for what he did in the end as long as he gives his life to Jesus."

"We do have to "pay" for it." Cody then gently pounded his fist on Wiebe's thigh saying, "We have two ways to do it for our transgression: we can die not having Jesus Christ as our Lord and Savior and pay for our sins with our own blood in Hell, which is what you said you wanted to do, or you can turn away from running your own life and rightfully trust your life to Jesus as your God and Savior using His blood through faith to "pay" for your sin, and receive Heaven."

"So it's not enough to ask Jesus to forgive me. He has to have complete control over my whole life?"

"Well, are you happy with the results of you being in charge thus far?"

Wiebe was silent for a good while as he looked back up at the sky. He wagged his head, and in a low voice replied, "No."

Another pause fell on them.

Cody felt the warm growth of the Holy Spirit's manifestation, particularly on Wiebe. He knew the Lord was putting the urge on Wiebe's heart to repent. "Jesus died and rose from the grave so that if you put your faith in Him your old ways will be put to death, and you will have a new life in obedience to him; a new start. God Himself will come and live in you, and empower you to grow in obedience to Him. But out of your own free will, through faith, you have to hand Him over the keys of your life."

"Is all this you're saying true?"

"God is truth. Jesus said He is the Way, the Truth, and the Life. But in the end, it's your decision that counts. God's grace will be irrelevant to you unless you choose to accept it."

Wiebe was pensive for a moment as the cool strong wind whirled into the tower. As it's thumping resonances left the chamber Wiebe returned his head to Cody's. "Should I do this now?"

"Yeah," answered Cody, "as soon as possible. Tomorrow's not guaranteed."

"What should I say to Him to be forgiven."

"What do you think you should say?"

"That I should ask Him for forgiveness, and for Him to have rule over my life."

Cody nodded his head. "Sounds good to me."

CHAPTER TWENTY SIX

Algoma, who was still praying with Lope, Nadie, and Corina, could not bear to pray for Wiebe anymore and she released her hands from them and turned to the screen.

"There's no need to pray for them anymore," said Algoma to everyone.

"What do you mean by that?" asked her mother.

As Lope, Corina, and Nadie stopped behind her, Algoma stood amazed, seeing Cody holding Wiebe by the shoulder as Wiebe himself, with his eyes closed, prayed.

After Wiebe said no more Cody opened his eyes. He then saw the man turn around and stand on the floor while unzipping himself out of his fire suit. Cody, though covered in his dark green leather jacket, felt cold for him seeing he was now only dressed in a tank top and boxers. Wiebe then used his suit for a towel wiping off the gasoline from his face and scalp. After throwing it to the floor he looked up to Cody.

Cody didn't notice a coldness in his eyes any more, but more of a stillness. It wasn't a look of withdrawal, but of one calmly taking everything in. Their silent exchange was a while as they just stood looking each other. Cody was now disturbed, for Wiebe's stare never left him. His pale blue eyes went through many changes, like seasons and winter seemed to be the transition they held fast to. An unfathomable since of regret tainted his eyes, and the Dark

Giant felt it. So strong, in fact, that it was as if the Holy Spirit had taken Wiebe's heart and grated against his own.

"I'm sorry for murdering your father." Choked Wiebe.

Cody was stunned. The most he expected to hear from this man just coming to Christ was thank you. But this was far more than he anticipated. Wiebe began to tear as guilt cloaked his face. When he tried hiding his face the tears broke through his fingers and his at first subtle whimpering started to become utterly bitter. Cody caught a glance of his knees starting to tremble. Fearing he needed catching, Cody immediately took his hands placing them on his shoulders. Wiebe's weeping grew stronger, and the stronger it grew Cody's spirit became more moved. Seeing him like this reminded the Dark Giant of the night he broke down before Lord confessing his selfishness. Tears now began to flow down the his face as well as something like a harden sludge melted within him. He then embraced his new brother.

"I forgive you." said Cody

Back at the Hotel Zur Burg Nurburg the Holy Spirit moved strongly on Michi in sight of this on the television screen. "Though I cannot see God I now know that He truly exists," he whispered to himself. He repeated this over and over as his eyes began to flood up with conviction, until he hurled his hands to the ceiling shouting, "Though I cannot see You, I know now that you really exist!!" As everyone in the room looked at him, Michi dropped to his knees doubled over while closing his eyes in prayer, and with arms still stretched out he trusted his life to Christ.

CHAPTER TWENTY SEVEN

Meanwhile, at the Celsos' house, Nadie sat down on the brown leather sofa beside a much distraught Algoma. She looked over to her daughter with that face of quiet inquisition.

"I feel like Jonah," answered her daughter, "and *Wiebe's* my Nineveh." She shook her head in disenchantment. "I know that God is merciful. I know that no one, including me, deserves His grace, but…" She paused while wiping away some tears. "I'm sorry, I just…Quite frankly I was really hoping that that skinny blonde crow would have really went through with what he said and lit himself to Hell." Her daughter looked over to her. "Why can you let it go, momma, and I can't?"

Nadie then looked to the screen, but her attention stayed on her daughter. "Well, from time to time my anger towards that man and what he did to Smoky left and returned here and there, especially during the early years after his death. But I was empowered through the Holy Spirit to obey Him and forgive, because I knew where your father was and I also knew that if the man who murdered him died he probably wouldn't be going to the same place. And just as God commanded me to forgive your grandfather, so must you heed God's command to forgive your father's murderer."

Nadie then gently laid her hand on her Algoma's. "Love holds no grudges 'Goma. You too, like that 'skinny blonde crow', were one of God's..."

"Objects of wrath," interjected Algoma, "before embracing His grace. I know that momma... I know."

"That's right. In everything you do in life your motive should always be to please your Father. You must not forgive Wiebe in means to make yourself feel better, but because it is commanded of *our* Father to forgive our transgressors; just as He forgives those who put their faith in Him, just as He forgave you."

Algoma sniffled as her violet eyes sparkled in fervor.

"Jesus," continued Nadie, "said that if you love Him you WILL," she firmly grasped hold of and gently shook her daughter's hand, "will obey His commandments. If you want to get closer to Christ and grow in obedience to Him, you're going to have to let go of your hatred towards this man and hand it over to Him. Then you will be free to forgive him."

Algoma's nodded in agreement. With that she bowed her head in prayer.

Back at the tower of the castle, Cody pulled away from Wiebe while holding him by the shoulders, "You know we're brothers now, right?"

"Brothers?" said Wiebe staring him strangely, while wiping away his tears.

"Yeah, man." As he put his hands back in his pockets he explained, "When we give our life to Jesus, He becomes our Father, and we become His children. So since we both now have the same Spiritual Father, we're now spiritual brothers."

"Hm," grunted Wiebe with a smirk. "Interesting."

"And I think my new brother could use a jacket. I know you're cold just being in your boxers and all."

"Oh. Ha." He then scratched his damp head while Cody took off his jacket. "Well you're talking to the idiot who once ran out at 10 below with less than this on in St. Petersburg, Russia."

"What in the world possessed you to do that?"

"I was 15." Wiebe shook his head in embarrassment while taking Cody's jacket from him. "It was some dumb dare from my racing academy mates at the time."

"Well, I just didn't want you to start off your new walk with Christ with hypothermia or pneumonia or something."

Wiebe was silent for a second as he slid into his new over-sized garment. His face then glowed in subtle excitement as he looked up at Cody. "Whether this walk starts off hot or cold," said Wiebe, "I'm sure with Jesus now at the helm, my horizon's going to be golden."

"Hm," grunted Cody with a smirk. He was deeply moved by Wiebe's epiphany, but out of insecurity he didn't want to reveal too much of its impact on his face. But, he then put his arm around his new brother's shoulder, and they both walked off towards the door that led down the tower.

www.ingramcontent.com/pod-product-compliance
Lightning Source LLC
Chambersburg PA
CBHW071925290426
44110CB00013B/1483